Thomas Barlow has been a [....] at Oxford University and at the Massachusetts Institute of Technology, a columnist with the Financial Times in London, and Scientific Advisor to the Minister for Education, Science and Training in the Australian Government. He currently works as an independent advisor to governments, universities, and other R&D-intensive organisations.

I0070682

Other books by Thomas Barlow

The Australian Miracle

BETWEEN THE EAGLE AND THE DRAGON

THOMAS BARLOW

B
―
A

First published 2013 by Barlow Advisory Pty Limited

Paperback edition ISBN 978-0-9871330-8-3
Digital (epub) edition ISBN 978-0-9871330-6-9
Digital (kindle) edition ISBN 978-0-9871330-7-6

Typesetting by Kirby Jones

Acknowledgements

This work was funded in part through the Merck Innovation Program at the United States Studies Centre at the University of Sydney.

Contents

Introduction

This book considers the intellectual and imaginative power of two great nations. In the coming decades, China is likely to overtake the US as the world's largest economy. Already a major force in global trade, the rise of China as an economic power has become a point of discussion in every corner of the developed world. At the same time, the recent financial crisis, which has shaken trust in the US economic model and left the US Government heavily indebted, appears to have bolstered confidence in China's future. Massive Chinese investments in infrastructure, especially educational infrastructure, and the growth of Chinese manufacturing firms are fostering a belief that China will soon match the US not only in the scale of its economy, but also as a powerhouse of science and innovation.

While the competitive threat that China poses to the US is an important consideration for all nations, the shifting dynamic between China and the US raises a special challenge for other countries in the Pacific. Many of these societies have deep and enduring links with America, ties that have been forged across economic, political, military and cultural dimensions. Yet many of these nations also possess historical, cultural and ethnic ties with China, and they now find themselves the beneficiaries of significant and swiftly expanding economic activity and trade links. Across the region, there is a mounting perception that China is rapidly supplanting the US as the land of opportunity.

As the balance of power shifts between these two great powers—the Eagle and the Dragon—many nations face a strategic dilemma. In most places, the choices are only beginning to be articulated. Can one take the US relationship for granted and focus on building new links with the emerging regional giant? Or do the tensions between one's strongest ally and one's largest trading partner signal that now is precisely the time to reaffirm ties with the US? For many countries these are essential questions and in answering them it's only natural to ponder which of these two nations will prove the greater power, technologically as well as economically. In a world that is changing so rapidly it seems wise to try to fathom which of these two great powers will come out on top. But as our title suggests these are different creatures with different strengths and the arena is vast, complex and uncertain.

Between the Eagle and the Dragon starts with

the premise that China's ability to challenge the US economically, militarily and politically will ultimately depend upon its capacity to replicate the levels of invention and innovation that exist across American society. It contrasts some of the basic elements of the American and Chinese innovation systems and confirms how rapidly China's scientific and technological capabilities have expanded over recent decades. Yet it also questions the perception that the world's intellectual centre of gravity is now heading unstoppably east, somewhere in the vicinity of Beijing.

1. The Great Rebalancing

The twentieth century is often referred to as the American century. In this century, it was the Americans who industrialised innovation. It was the Americans who launched new global industries based on novel technologies such as the internal combustion engine, motion pictures, aerospace, television, plastics, electronics, computer software, biotechnology and the Internet. Many of the defining technological achievements of our time have been American. The transistor, the mobile phone, the contraceptive pill and genetic engineering were all originally developed in the US. Indeed, during the twentieth century, Americans redefined the scale of human technological ambition. The US was the first nation to develop a nuclear weapon. The US led the landmark project to sequence the human genome, pioneering another new frontier. Fifty years on, the US remains the only nation to have put men on the moon and brought them back again.

The influence of American technological creativity on human civilisation is without precedent. There is a view, however, that the US is now in a state of relative decline. Today it has become a platitude to speak of the coming century as the Asian century or even as the Chinese century. Notions of imminent Chinese supremacy are increasingly common, almost taken for granted. For thirty years, the Chinese economy has been booming. The Chinese have become voracious consumers of the world's commodities. Consumers everywhere else are buying Chinese manufactured goods in unprecedented volumes. Vast numbers of visitors to China have felt for themselves the excitement and dynamism that exists now in many Chinese cities. The number and affluence of Chinese tourists travelling abroad has also increased. Right across the world, there is an acute awareness of growing Chinese wealth and power.

Upon first consideration, these trends suggest that the world is changing in a fundamental way. Extrapolating directly from the pattern of the past thirty years implies that the US is now destined to account for an ever-declining share of world economic activity into the foreseeable future. It also suggests an altogether brighter future for China. But does it imply a shifting balance in the relative technological competitiveness of China and the US? China's emergence as a leading exporter of high-technology manufactured products seems to suggest that such a transition is already underway. Moreover, a link is often observed between a society's economic performance and its underlying capacity for innovation. The natural assumption then is that the Chinese are broadly on the ascendant and that their triumphant eclipsing of American technological and innovative capabilities is only a matter of time.

Addressing this assumption is the purpose of this book. Our thesis is that China is unlikely to supplant the US any time soon as the world's dominant driver of technological ingenuity. But we begin by noting that perceptions of determinism about the rise of China and the decline of the US are entirely understandable.

1.1 China appears to be a land of economic opportunity

First, it should be said that China's metamorphosis from an impoverished, agrarian state to an economic and technological superpower looks increasingly like the consequence of an inexorable process. Thirty years ago, the Chinese economy was less than a tenth the size of the American economy. China's economy was in fact scarcely much larger than Australia's—a staggering comparison given the relative scale of the populations in these two nations. Yet official growth in the Chinese economy has subsequently averaged 10% annually. Over the past two decades, growth in China's international trade in goods and services has averaged more than 15% annually. Consequently, China is already an economic superpower. Its economy is now the world's second largest and its recent trajectory clearly suggests that it won't be long before it supersedes the American economy in scale (WEO 2011).

Some people like to question the validity of these statistics. For a variety of reasons, measures of gross domestic product cannot be considered very reliable in China's case. However, there are other ways to characterise the scale of the Chinese transformation, and few metrics are more interesting in this respect than those relating to electricity production. Analogous to the growth of its economy, China has experienced exponential expansion in electricity production over recent decades compared with the linear growth that has occurred in the US, Europe, and Japan. In the early 1970s, China produced electricity at around the same order of magnitude as Australia. By the mid-1990s, China had begun producing electricity on a greater scale than Japan, and today it produces electricity on a scale greater than Europe (WB 2011). By this particular measure, China looks likely to overtake the US within a decade.

Furthermore, since electricity drastically increases the opportunities for both consumers and producers to innovate, this transition implies much more than just economic development. Energy use is a defining feature of all human civilisations and the development of electric power generation was a key precursor for a vast range of innovations in developed nations during the twentieth century. Without the ubiquitous distribution of reliable electric power, it is difficult to imagine the subsequent development of refrigerators, televisions, computers, or mobile telephones. Electric power has also come to play an important role in manufacturing innovation. For example, the Bessemer process for making steel was first patented in the 1850s but needed the low-cost electricity of the twentieth century to make it practical (Mowery 1998). Electricity production is not just an important proxy for economic activity. It can also be seen as an essential precursor determining a society's innovative potential.

A second critique of any comparison based solely on gross domestic product stems from the view that one cannot ascertain the success or the creativity of an economy from its scale alone. According to this argument, even when national figures relating to gross domestic product are accurate, they can mislead. According to this critique, what counts is not what a society produces in aggregate, but the extent to which a society utilises resources productively. This can be measured by normalising the scale of an economy against the size of its population.

If one pursues such an approach, the gulf in capability between the developed world and China remains very large indeed. Comparing China's economic activity per capita with that of developed nations reveals that, although the Chinese economy has surged over recent years, it is still far from maximising the economic potential of its human capital. In 2010, China's gross domestic product per capita was still less than a third of the European Union's, less than a quarter of Japan's or Australia's, and less than a fifth that of America's (WEO 2011). In other words, economic activity per capita in China still lags behind that of developed economies and, while China may well be poised to become a larger economy than the US in the short term, it would seem it still has a long way to go before it will match the US in sophistication and efficiency, and by implication in creativity and innovation.

There is considerable merit in this argument. As we shall see, China's per capita economic activity does provide a fair reflection of China's innovative capability in aggregate. However, the problem in evaluating a large and complex nation like China is that national data can hide considerable regional variation. A low level of national output per capita may obscure a high level of output in a particular region or city. Economic output per capita and the evidence for innovation in China are certainly not uniform across the country. Furthermore, so long as China's economy continues to grow at an elevated rate, its per-capita activity will gradually converge with that of developed nations.

Indeed, China's low level of per-capita activity is frequently used to justify favourable expectations about the Chinese economy and about Chinese innovation over the long term.

Consider that even today, with a population over four times that of the US, China has only as many registered motor vehicles as there were in the US back in the early 1950s (WB 2011 and Mowery 1999). China's total road network, on a kilometre basis, grew fourfold between 1980 and 2008, and yet at the end of this period China still had less than two thirds of the road network in the US. As recently as 2008, China's total rail network (measured in kilometres of track) was still less than a third the size of that in the US. China's land area is similar to that of the US, although with much greater population density, and yet there are still over three times as many aircraft passengers travelling internally in the US each year than in China (WB 2011).

China clearly has the potential to persist for a long time as a land of economic opportunity. Given the dazzling growth of the past thirty years and the evident opportunities for ongoing industrialisation, it seems perfectly credible to assume that China will continue inexorably to expand both the size of its economy and its economic output per capita. It also seems plausible to imagine that these developments will steadily enhance the technological competitiveness of Chinese businesses.

1.2 China is already competing with the US in high-technology manufacturing

Japan, South Korea and Taiwan have all demonstrated the ability of emerging economies to link economic development to a dramatic expansion in technological capability. The precedent set by these East Asian nations during the latter half of the last century helps to convey a further sense of inevitability about the rise of China's technological capability, not least since China has already emerged as a leading manufacturer and exporter of information and communications products. Official trade statistics show a meteoric rise in China's recent exports of information and communications technology goods by value. Over the first decade of the twenty-first century, Chinese exports of such goods exploded from roughly half the value of similar US exports in 2000 to around three times the value of US exports a decade later (NSF 2010 and OECD MSTI). This confirms what everybody knows from direct experience: there has been a proliferation of electronic gadgets whose production is finalised in China. The motto engraved on the back of every iPhone says it all: "Designed by Apple in California. Assembled in China."

Contemporary trade data do have some well-known limitations. Many nations can be involved in the value chain of high-technology manufactured goods—a fact omitted from the trade statistics. Globalisation means that goods can be designed in one country, manufactured using components from several different countries, then assembled in a separate country before being finally sold somewhere else. This pattern has particular relevance for China. For the most part, China's exports are not manufactured from scratch. They are often assembled from imported components and the flow of value is further complicated by foreign ownership patterns among Chinese firms.

Factors such as these should make one circumspect when interpreting trade figures. One recent study has suggested that domestic value-adding activity accounts for just 15% of the return from China's electronic and information technology exports (Branstetter 2008). Research into the global value chain in the production of the iPod, the iPhone and the iPad reiterates this analysis. These "iProducts" are all assembled in China and contribute to the US-China trade deficit to the tune of $150 per unit for the iPod, $229 per unit for the iPhone, and $275 per unit for the iPad. Yet the value captured in China from the sale of these devices is estimated at only around $10 per unit, with some returns flowing to component-makers in Japan, Taiwan and South Korea, but with by far the largest returns actually retained by Apple back in America (Dedrick 2008, Kraemer 2011).

Given that the trade data are not easy to interpret, it makes sense to look for alternative representations of the global distribution of high-technology manufacturing. One such approach is to calculate high-technology manufacturing activity in different countries as a share of global industry value added. Analysis along these lines shows that while China has indeed rapidly increased its global share of high-technology manufacturing activity, displacing Japanese share, surprisingly it has not significantly affected European or American share (NSF 2010). Contrary to what one might conclude from export data, this does not imply a sharp escalation in indigenous Chinese high-technology industry. Rather it is consistent with the thesis that manufacturers from other parts of Asia have simply been relocating labour-intensive aspects of their business to China.

On this basis, technological triumphalism about China would seem premature. However, the significance of Chinese achievement should not be underestimated. There is evidence that China's exports on the whole are growing in technological sophistication over time (Schott 2008 and Wang 2010). China's exports have included a steadily increasing research and development (R&D) intensity from the 1980s to the present (Brandt 2008). Across a range of industries there is also strong evidence of productivity growth in China. Between 1978 and 2005, output per worker in the Chinese steel industry rose tenfold, much faster than the growth in the developed world, with leading Chinese firms now approaching the productivity norms of their competitors in developed countries both in terms of labour and input productivity (Brandt 2008).

These are all positive trends, but perhaps the most important development for China is the bare fact of its growing involvement in manufacturing supply chains. Chinese firms now play a key global role in manufacturing an extraordinarily wide range of products. Yes, China may be some way off from being a genuine challenger to US pre-eminence in the invention, design, and production of many high-technology goods but it has clearly established itself in a critical role. Businesses learn to innovate by doing. The scale of competition in Chinese manufacturing seems highly likely to induce ongoing learning and innovation within many Chinese businesses. Given the history of Japan and South Korea, and given the potential scale of the Chinese economy, the view that China will some day overtake the US as the world's leading technological power is very easy to comprehend. Such a view can seem almost ineluctable.

1.3 Is it inevitable that the world's largest economy will become its most innovative?

This brings us to a pivotal theme. Determinism about China's transformation into a technological superpower is ultimately predicated not only upon China's track record of economic growth and its budding manufacturing capabilities; equally crucial is the belief that China's economic scale will of itself enable rapid development of advanced scientific and technological capabilities. This principle has been frequently demonstrated in the past, including by the US, most visibly with the Manhattan project and the Apollo missions, but also in the commercial sphere. A society's capacity for making all kinds of investments in new technologies, science and innovation is highly influenced by the size of its economy. Opportunities for innovation do not just grow naturally with the size of markets, the scale of the workforce, or the magnitude of available capital. On the contrary, big economies have disproportionately large advantages in fostering innovation across each of these dimensions.

First, the larger a market, the greater the potential returns from a new innovation. All other things being equal, larger markets tend to justify more substantial investments in the development of new products or processes than do smaller markets. In other words, larger markets can enable deeper and riskier forms of innovation than smaller markets. This effect helps explain why Hollywood makes such expensive feature films compared with the film industries in other nations, and why Hollywood products in turn tend to dominate global box office sales. It also explains why a significant proportion of the world's development of new pharmaceuticals occurs in the US.

Second, the larger an economy's workforce, the greater will be its number of potential inventors, innovators, and entrepreneurs; and again, this advantage is not merely proportional. Larger economies have the potential to support larger and more diverse creative communities than smaller economies. Within these communities, larger economies have greater scope for labour specialisation and hence for the implementation of innovations that depend on labour specialisation. In addition, the tendency of talented people to seek out their own kind and to compete with their own kind strongly favours larger societies over smaller ones. In a world of easy migration, large economies have disproportionate attractions for foreign innovators who wish to live and work with like-minded people. All other things being equal, a larger society is more likely than a smaller society to win Nobel Prizes or nurture truly great business leaders.

Third, large economies have a unique capacity to pool capital, and the globalisation of capital does not invalidate this propensity. Obviously some forms of innovation benefit from concentrations of investment. A large economy will find it easier to channel capital into major public scientific infrastructure (such as telescopes or particle accelerators) than a small economy, which may instead seek international agreements to access such facilities built elsewhere, or which may be compelled to co-operate with other nations in the building of such facilities. A large economy can invest a heady amount by global standards into one university without also jeopardising its capacity to run a large number of other high quality institutions. Investment in venture projects will also tend to be much more versatile in a large economy than in a small economy. Large economies can pool capital in more diverse ways and thereby respond to a greater range of opportunities than is possible in small economies.

Given the importance of economic scale in establishing an advantage in innovation, the current rebalancing of the world economy would seem a momentous development. For over a century, American innovators have benefited from the scale of their domestic market, the size of their workforce, and their ability to pool capital. But these advantages are eroding. The US has accounted for a steadily declining share of the global economy for years and in the coming decades, for the first time in the modern era, it could face a competitor with an economy larger than its own.

In this context, it ought to be acknowledged that declines in American competitiveness in science, technology and innovation are by no means predestined. Smaller economies have been known to outperform larger economies across each of these dimensions. Nor is it inevitable that China's economy will eclipse that of the US. Other Asian nations have experienced a steady slowing of growth rates as they developed. This has been true of Japan, Taiwan, South Korea and Hong Kong, and there has been no shortage of commentary suggesting that China's growth will also stall. The most pessimistic assessments highlight the problems inherent in China's tradition of authoritarian government, in its dependence upon fixed-capital investment, in the excessive power of its bureaucrat capitalists, in the vulnerabilities of its banking system, and in its widespread corruption, inequality, and lack of political freedom. (See for example Jenner 1994, Lee 2007, Hutton 2008.)

These are all sound reasons to temper projections about China's future potential and the relative demise of the US. Nonetheless, the logic connecting economic scale and innovative capacity creates a powerful perception. Despite the uncertainties, it remains extremely likely that China will eventually become a greater economic force than the US and it remains perfectly rational to imagine that China's economic scale will, in turn, engender an unmatchable technological prowess. It is not unreasonable at all to argue that it is only a matter of time before China assumes the mantle not only of the world's largest but also of the world's most innovative economy.

1.4 The Western Pacific is a region caught in the shifting balance of power

China's rise and the rebalancing of economic activity across the Pacific have provoked ambivalence in many nations. The cheap goods generated by China's low labour costs and its growing participation in global trade have clearly brought benefits to the citizens of many countries. Few would begrudge the reduction in poverty that has occurred for large numbers of Chinese. But there is widespread concern about the costs that accompany these benefits.

There is a fear, for example, that China's expansion is threatening the competitiveness of businesses based in the developed world and that jobs, including jobs in high-technology industries, are being threatened. There is also a growing anxiety that organisations in the West are either missing opportunities in China or—worse still—rushing to seize opportunities and getting burned in the process. Those seeking to maximise their exposure to China's growth have frequently found risks and unforeseen costs in doing so. More serious, of course, are the security implications of China's rise. In the years ahead, it is likely that advances in Chinese military technology will enable China to threaten US strategic dominance in the Pacific. This may serve to destabilise international politics across the region. Certainly as America's share of the global economy shrinks and as China's expands, this part of the world suddenly seems a much less predictable place.

In light of these developments, while ambivalence about the rise of China exists in many different parts of the world, these issues seem especially acute in the Western Pacific. Here more than a dozen nations (including Indonesia, Japan, the Philippines, Vietnam, Thailand, South Korea, Taiwan, Malaysia, Australia and New Zealand) lie within China's growing sphere of influence. Many also have longstanding relationships with the US. For some of these nations, the changes of recent decades have been largely positive. Australia, for example, has longstanding and powerful cultural, political, and commercial connections with the US; but now it also has a complementary trading relationship with China and stands to benefit from a growing network of Chinese immigrants and Chinese graduates from Australian universities. Culturally and linguistically, innovative Australians are increasingly well equipped to connect with both powers.

By comparison, Japan's benefits from the growth of China are not so decisive. Historical tensions, disputed territories and antagonism around intellectual property rights have muddied Japan's relationship with its large neighbour. Yet even in this case, there have been some important and obvious advantages from the rise of the Dragon: China supplies Japanese firms with cheap labour, the Chinese economy has already evolved into an important consumer of Japanese products and China is now Japan's largest trading partner. Moreover, none of this has occurred to the detriment of Japan's relationship with the US. Japan and the US remain key trading partners with shared democratic values and common security objectives.

Other countries have faced their own set of tensions as they adapt to this regional shift in economic activity. Generally these issues have proved manageable. The growth of the Chinese economy has been essentially positive: it has expanded the range of commercial opportunities available across the Pacific without jeopardising valuable relationships with American partners; but this situation may not last. All countries across the region face potential trade offs as they seek to align their interests with those of both the current power and the emerging power. Culturally, economically and geographically, the circumstances of Western Pacific nations render them especially sensitive to the growing competition between the US and China. There will be instances where choices must be made: difficult choices in which individuals or organisations have to choose one partner over the other.

Neither the US nor China will render such choices easy. As perceptions about market opportunity and technological creativity shift, there is already a growing competitive tension between these two powers. This tension has been moderated in the past by the interdependency of the Chinese and American economies: the US and China do share one of the world's great bilateral trade partnerships. However as China's economy grows and as its technological competitiveness increases, the relative significance of this interdependency will diminish and the sense of international contest will mount. The Pacific is a region where American and Chinese rivalry looks set to escalate.

Under such circumstances, knowing which power to side with becomes a key challenge. The difficulties are obvious. It is no longer certain that the US will find a way to leverage its values and culture in order to re-energise its economy and maintain its status as the world's major generator of new technologies and ideas. Nor is it inevitable that China will continue its recent momentum and complete the transition from a society that is catching up to one that is a technological leader. Given all the uncertainties, an evidence-based evaluation of how things currently stand seems worthwhile.

Those societies that now find themselves caught between the Eagle and the Dragon are not merely passive bystanders to some external historical horserace over which they have no influence. How the nations of the Western Pacific place their bets, how they respond to the competing demands and trajectories of both the major powers will itself help to determine the outcome, together with the security and prosperity of the region. Whether the twenty-first century will indeed be the Chinese century or whether it will prove to be yet another American century is a defining question for our time.

2. The Eagle

When Steve Jobs, the founder and CEO of Apple, died on the fifth of October in 2011 his company had become the world's most valuable publicly traded firm. Less than a year later, on the seventeenth of May in 2012, another American technology company, Facebook, listed on the NASDAQ stock market, reaching an initial (and albeit temporary) valuation of $104 billion: a record figure for a newly listed company. American society clearly retains an extraordinary capacity to marry technological achievement with commercial outcomes. Yet there is evidence that the US position is weakening. Several measures of innovation performance indicate a startling decline in the scale and status of US innovation relative to the rest of the world. The evidence for American leadership is not as decisive as it was ten years ago. It is possible that the American age of innovation has already passed its zenith.

Consider the following provocative developments. First, there is the downward trend in R&D investment.

In the mid-1990s, the US accounted for nearly half of business R&D activity across all developed nations plus China. A decade later, its share of activity across these same nations had fallen to less than 40% (OECD MSTI). Second, there is the waning of US representation among leading innovative companies. As recently as 2005, the US accounted for over 40% of the leading 1000 corporations globally by expenditure on R&D. Yet by 2009, within just four years, its share had declined to a third of the global total (DIUS 2011). Third, there is the contraction in the US share of high-technology patents. In the early 1990s, the US accounted for over half the world's patent applications made through the Patent Cooperation Treaty (PCT) in high-technology areas like biotechnology and information and communications technology. Today, its share of PCT patents in these same high-technology areas has dropped to a third of world totals (OECD PD). Fourth, there is a diminution of American scientific productivity relative to the rest of the world. In the mid-1990s, the US accounted for more than a third of the world's scientific publications. Fifteen years later, its researchers were responsible for just 26.5% of global scientific outputs across all fields in aggregate, and for only 16.5% of the world's articles in physics and chemistry (NSF 2012).

A nation's potential for technological innovation can manifest itself in various ways. The developments described above are based upon four imperfect measures. Technological innovation can occur without formal R&D investment. Innovation may be more likely to emerge in small companies than in large ones. Patents are employed with varying enthusiasm across different industrial sectors and applicants in different nations are known to follow remarkably diverse patenting strategies. The relationship between scientific output and technological advantage is never straightforward.

While these measures may not be perfect, however, it does not follow that they are useless. R&D investment, the role of large companies, the level of patenting activity, and scientific productivity are all potent indicators of technological potential. This is especially true for economies with a substantial high-technology component. For this reason, the developments cited above must be taken seriously. Furthermore, these indicators seem to convey a consistent message: they reveal a trajectory of decline, they imply a downgrading of creative and technological power relative to other nations; they seem to support the hypothesis that an ascendant China will eventually supplant the US in technological capability.

Nevertheless, one should resist drawing hasty conclusions. Before the nations of the world unhitch their wagons from the train of American progress, it is worth exploring some of these trends in a more nuanced way. As we shall see, the US is still the unequivocal leader in industrial R&D, in the number of large innovative firms, in global patenting, and in scientific discovery, and it can be expected to retain this leadership for decades to come.

2.1 The US is still the leader in industrial research and development

For twenty years from the early 1990s, China, the US and most other developed nations steadily increased spending on industrial R&D. However growth has been much faster in some regions than in others. As a consequence, the US, Japan and Europe all experienced a decline in their share of industrial R&D activity relative to other developed nations and China. This shift was partly due to impressive activity in smaller OECD countries like Australia and South Korea, both of which experienced extremely strong growth in industrial R&D investment over the past two decades. Consistent with external impressions though, China has been the key player.

At the start of the 1990s, Chinese business expenditures on R&D were less than 1% of those across the developed nations plus China. Two decades later, China accounted for 15% of total business R&D expenditures across these same nations (OECD MSTI). This establishes the speed of the recent growth in business innovation investment in China and it illustrates the impact of this growth on the relative share of business R&D occurring in all the large developed economies. But it also points unexpectedly to the enduring strength of the US, at least for the time being.

Over the decade to 2008, China's share of business R&D in the OECD plus China rose by just one percentage point per annum, while the US's share fell by an average of 0.7 percentage points per annum. Were such a trend to continue, China would overtake the US in business R&D investment by 2025. However, as the Chinese economy gets bigger, it is likely that its rate of economic growth will be tempered, and it is by no means assured that Chinese firms will continue to increase their spending on R&D at the current rate over such a period. Thus even a generation hence, the world's dominant investor in business R&D is still likely to be America.

The US is also likely to remain a high-intensity investor, as US businesses continue to invest disproportionately large amounts in R&D relative to their scale of operation. Relative to the size of its economy, Americans spend nearly 80% more on industrial R&D than either the Chinese or the Europeans. Indeed, for many years there has been more reason for concern about the diminishing competitive advantage in Europe than in the US. As a share of their economy, European businesses invest less in R&D than Australian businesses, and only marginally more than

Chinese businesses (OECD MSTI). On this basis it can be argued that Europe is much more vulnerable to the competitive threat from Chinese innovation than is America. For the time being, despite its diminishing share of total global activity, the US is still easily the global leader in business R&D investment and looks likely to maintain this dominance relative to all other nations for many years to come.

2.2 The US is still the leader in innovative companies

Turning to the geographic distribution of large corporations, another interesting picture emerges. Over the first decade of the twenty-first century, the US share of the world's leading 1000 corporations by spending on R&D shrank to a point where it started to seem low relative to total US business R&D investment. By comparison, relative to their overall investment in business R&D, Japan and Europe both now have a higher share of the top 1000 companies. To put this in perspective, in 2009 despite its much weaker overall investment in business R&D, Europe accounted for nearly the same number of companies as the US on the top 1000 list (DIUS 2011 and OECD MSTI).

This implies that business R&D is less concentrated within America's largest-spending corporations than is true in either Japan or Europe. Such a disparity seems to be a fairly recent phenomenon. Of the top 1000 companies globally, as ranked by R&D expenditure, the proportion that have been based in the US dropped noticeably between 2005 and 2009. This may signal a healthy diversification in uncertain times, a beneficial spreading of the risks involved in R&D investments throughout the US economy. But it also suggests that in a great number of sectors American firms have reduced their historical prominence as top individual investors in the discovery and exploitation of new knowledge. Traditionally, large firms have been responsible for the vast majority of R&D investment globally. A declining American share of the world's firms with the biggest R&D budgets could be interpreted as a leading indicator of an approaching decline in overall US business investment in this area. Yet such a claim would seem overly bold. It is just as likely that large US firms are spearheading a global shift towards outsourcing many of their innovative activities, including R&D, to smaller, more agile, and more risk-compatible organisations (Chesbrough 2003). So long as overall R&D investment remains strong, the shrinking American share of the top 1000 firms by R&D spending may even be a sign of American versatility and innovation. Most significantly for our story, US representation on this list is certainly not shrinking due to the growth of Chinese firms.

With some fascinating exceptions, Chinese firms have not yet established much visibility on this top

1000 list. In 2009, Chinese firms accounted for only 2% of companies listed (DIUS 2011). There are many plausible explanations. Finding sound financial information on individual Chinese companies is often challenging. It is possible that business R&D activity in China may be spread across a relatively large number of companies. It is also conceivable that much of the R&D activity in China is being funded from off shore, perhaps by American, Japanese or Taiwanese firms. Whatever the explanation, it is firms not in China but in other developed countries that continue, for the time being, to provide the main competition in R&D for large American corporations.

2.3 The US is still the leader in global patenting activity

According to private R&D investment patterns, the US remains strong in technological innovation relative to China. But how does this compare with international patenting activity? Investment in R&D provides a measure of a nation's capability for improving or generating new technologies. Patents are another possible measure of this capability. Analysing patents provides some indication of the technological sophistication of an economy and of its likely potential for generating future prosperity specifically from intellectual property.

As mentioned earlier, patents are not a perfect measure. While they tend to be most significant in high-technology industries, it is not possible to derive the value of a patent portfolio based solely on the quantity of patents within it. Nonetheless patents do highlight trends in rational and verifiable ways: when Japanese industry began competing directly with US firms in high-technology areas, Japan's share of global patents rose dramatically. Since patents are classified into a range of technological classes, they are also useful in determining an economy's technological orientation.

In the following assessments we use data on international patents filed under the Patent Cooperation Treaty (PCT). The PCT data are useful in making international comparisons, as there is no home country bias of the kind one observes in data derived from national or regional patenting offices. A higher proportion of PCT patents may also be relevant to a more diverse set of regional markets than is true for patents filed directly through national offices. In other words, patents channelled through the PCT system may, on average, have greater commercial value than patents pursued directly through national offices.

Examining the PCT data, it should be acknowledged that the US is still the dominant nation by share of global activity. However, consistent with the evidence on R&D investment, recent trends in patent applications through the PCT system suggest a decline in the relative importance of American invention. The gap between the US and the rest of the world has narrowed. The US and Europe both show a steadily declining share of PCT patents since the mid-1990s.

In part, this shift can be explained by the growth in PCT applications emanating from Japan and, to a lesser extent, South Korea. Contrary to what one might expect then, the balance in patenting activity cannot yet be attributed exclusively to China. Quite surprisingly, PCT patenting activity from China only exceeded that of Australia in 2004. China is rapidly increasing its patenting activity, especially in its domestic market, but it was only in 2009 that China for the first time accounted for a greater number of PCT patent filings than South Korea or France (OECD PD). China is not yet operating on a scale even remotely comparable to the US, Japan or Europe as a whole.

Furthermore, trends of total activity obscure what may be happening in specific areas of invention. Historically, the US has had a particular strength in many areas of advanced technology. Over the three years from 1990 to 1992, the US accounted for 44% of all PCT patent applications, but for a remarkable 53% of patent applications in biotechnology and information and communications technology. Relative to other nations, this focus on high-technology areas has since eroded, although the evidence here is nuanced depending upon the technology area.

For instance, over the three years to 2009, the US accounted for just 29% of world PCT patent filings and for a merely proportionate 30% of filings in information and communications technology. This remained a greater share than that of Europe (24%), Japan (21%), or China (7%), but evidently the gap between the US and the rest of the world in this technological domain has contracted. China, in particular, increased its share of global PCT filings in this area more than tenfold over the course of the decade.

However, this only holds for information and communications technology. By contrast the US has preserved its clear dominance in biotechnology, accounting for 42% of global PCT filings in this domain, a share equivalent to that of Europe, Japan and China combined. Indeed, between 2007 and 2009, China accounted for just 2% of global PCT applications relating to biotechnology, a share on par with Australia (OECD PD).

Firstly, one should observe that this evidence of technological decline is once again greater for Europe than for the US. American inventors still retain a much stronger focus on advanced technology than their European competitors. In the early 1990s, Europeans accounted for a third of PCT applications for patents relating to either information and communications technology or biotechnology. Their share since declined to less than a quarter. Likewise, only a third of PCT applications by European inventors are focused on information and communications technology or biotechnology, compared with nearly a half for the US, Japan and China.

Secondly, it is clear that the erosion of US dominance specifically in the area of information and communications technology has been strongly determined by inventive competition from Asia as a whole, rather than China specifically. This being understood, information and communications technology still constitutes a flashpoint for US-Chinese competition. The US currently has less focus (i.e. a lower proportion of its total PCT applications) in this area than China, and China's success in accelerating its share of PCT filings in this area over the past decade shows how rapidly a country's position can change. While US inventors will no doubt remain predominant by scale of patenting activity for many years, it is reasonable to project an ongoing reduction in America's share of global patent applications and an ongoing rise in China's share into the future.

Finally, given the proclamations now regularly made about the importance of clean energy technology, it is worth commenting on the breakdown of PCT applications in this area. Renewable energy technology has become associated with various techno-utopian fantasies in recent years. It is an area where commercial success depends as much upon political intervention in energy markets as upon inventive capacity. Perhaps as a consequence, the level of global patenting activity does not correlate with the hype one often hears about this technology. Renewable and non-fossil fuel energy technologies accounted for less than 3% of PCT applications in 2009. Despite its topicality, this remains an emerging but modest area of technological innovation.

Interestingly, European inventors are strongest in this category, though the overall figures hide considerable variations across different forms of non-fossil fuel energy technologies. Japan accounts for a high share of PCT applications in solar photovoltaic energy and fuel cell technologies, while Europe accounts for a high share of PCT applications in wind energy, hydro energy, solar thermal energy, and fuel from waste technologies (WIPO 2010 and OECD PD). The US has its greatest relative strengths in geothermal energy, solar photovoltaic energy, and in biofuels and fuel from waste technologies. By contrast, there is no obvious evidence that China has developed a strong inventive position in any of these areas. Overall, China accounted for only 3% of global PCT filings relating to renewable energy technology between 2007 and 2009. If the Chinese are leading in innovation in this area it is by developing cost-efficient manufacturing processes of existing technologies rather than by advancing solar energy technologies per se.

It is impossible to determine the value of each nation's patent portfolio from international patent statistics. Grand-scale patent productivity is not necessarily a guarantee of future profits. A large number of patents will ultimately find no application and have little value, while a few patents will usually prove to be enormously valuable. However, it is possible to draw some conclusions from the international patent data. On the one hand, the US still clearly remains the dominant producer of technological innovation globally and seems likely to remain so for the foreseeable future. On the other hand, its lead looks to be narrowing steadily, not so much because of a US decline but because of the vigour of its emerging competitors in Asia. Asian business investment in R&D and Asian inventiveness in information and communications technologies are key factors.

Surprisingly, given the level of public attention that has been focused on China in recent years, China's impact in this respect has been important but not overwhelming. There is evidence of growing technological innovation in China, but not yet on a scale to match that in Japan, let alone in the US. Nonetheless, the sense of American vulnerability on this score will likely become more acute if the Chinese economy continues to grow, and if the world economy continues to nurture Chinese businesses that are active and successful in high-technology sectors.

2.4 The US is still the leader in scientific discovery

This brings us to the evidence of relative decline in the standing of American science. The relationship between scientific and technological innovation is rarely straightforward. Advances in science have sometimes assisted technological advances in industry and sometimes they have driven the creation of entirely new industries, as was the case with biotechnology and electricity. But advances in technology have also had profound impacts upon science. Developments in instrumentation, for example, have proved essential for many great discoveries: a pattern that extends from Galileo and his telescope through to modern geneticists' reliance on microarray chips and supercomputers.

Science and technology are mutually reinforcing. In general, the more a community understands about one of these two domains, the greater its potential to advance the other. And yet there is an imperfect relationship between different nations' technological sophistication and their levels of scientific success. The Greeks may have squared the hypotenuse and foreshadowed the discovery of the atom, but it was the Romans who built the roads, bridges and viaducts of Europe. While British men like Thomas Newcomen and James Watt made the steam engine work in practice, it was a Frenchman Sadi Carnot who figured out how it worked in theory. While the Germans in the early twentieth century were winning a disproportionately large number of Nobel Prizes, it was the Americans who were mass-producing motorcars.

One exceptional attribute of American society in the latter half of the twentieth century was its global dominance in both technological and scientific innovation. Following the success of major scientific projects during the Second World War, and driven in part by the unusual role played by the scientific community during the Cold War, the US massively increased its public investments in scientific research. From the 1950s through to the present, the US has leveraged its economic power, its technological prowess, and its attraction as a destination for skilled migrants and university graduate students, in order to build an unprecedented capability in science.

The evidence for this is remarkable. Between 1951 and 2000, US residents accounted for 58% of Nobel Laureates in the sciences, compared with 13% for the UK, 7% for Germany, 2% for Japan, and 1% for China (Nobel 2008). In addition, the US dominates most international rankings of universities. In 2012, the Academic Ranking of World Universities run by the Shanghai Jiao Tong University ranked 53 US institutions among the top 100 universities worldwide (SJTU 2012). For decades, scientists based in the US have dominated the scientific literature globally. It is the success of American research, rather than British research, that has steadily rendered English the *lingua franca* of the global scientific community.

American researchers have long published a disproportionately large share of articles relative to researchers in other nations and have had their research referenced even more disproportionately within the global scientific literature—although this may now be changing. Research articles published in scientific journals have been indexed over many years by Thomson Reuters. The Thomson Reuters' Science Citation Index reveals that the US accounted for 26% of global scientific articles in 2009, down from 34% in 1995. But again this is a trend that should be interpreted cautiously: despite its declining share of global activity, the US remains the dominant force in scientific research; no other nation in that year exceeded 10% of the world's scientific literature. The data also imply that the US is not yet threatened, at least in an imminent sense, by the rapid growth in China's scientific production. By 2009 China accounted for just over 9% of the world's scientific articles, the second highest level of production of any nation, greater than Japan or Germany or the UK, but still significantly lower than the US share (NSF 2012).

This noted, there is little rationale for American complacency because the aggregated data across all fields hide an important development that emerges when one breaks down levels of national output according to specific fields. China has a rather different focus in its public research portfolio than the US. Consequently, in some fields there is already near-comparability in the scale of Chinese and American outputs. For example, if one traces the trends in scientific publications in the fields of chemistry and physics, then it becomes apparent that China is poised to overtake the US within just a few years, if it has not already done so. In 2009 China accounted for 16.2% of global outputs in these fields, up from less than 5% in the mid-1990s. This compares with a US share of 16.5%, down from 22% in the mid-1990s (NSF 2012).

A similar trend occurs in the fields of engineering, mathematics and computer sciences. In these fields there remains a slightly bigger gap between the Chinese and American levels of output, but again it is a gap that appears to be closing rapidly. In 2009 the US accounted for 20% of global outputs in these three fields, compared with 15% for China (NSF 2012). Based on recent trends, one would anticipate convergence in scale of activity within a decade. Among these three fields it should be noted that this sense of convergence is particularly acute in engineering and mathematics, with a slightly slower up-kick in China's recent output in computer sciences.

Analysis of trends in physics, chemistry and engineering presents a much more sobering conclusion for the US than would be deduced from an assessment of total research outputs across all fields. And yet, the corollary of this is a much less pronounced convergence in other areas. In recent years, there has been only a modest decline in the American share of scientific outputs in biological, medical and other life sciences matched by only moderate growth in China's global share of activity in these fields. In 2009 the US accounted for 32% of global publications in life sciences, compared with just 5% for China. In psychology and the social sciences the disparity between the US and the rest of the world is more striking still, although this may well be influenced by a language bias in the selection of journals that constitute the Thomson Reuters dataset.

In general we can say that the US strength in science is looking increasingly lopsided. There is a strong distinction between the physical, life and social sciences. Like Japan and other emerging Asian nations, China has prioritised investment in the physical sciences, while the US has recently prioritised investment in the biological and life sciences. In 2009, 46% of China's scientific publications were in chemistry or physics, while 24% were in agricultural, biological, medical or other life sciences. By comparison, 17% of US outputs were in chemistry or physics, while 57% were in agricultural, biological, medical or other life sciences (NSF 2012). The US still dominates by volume of scientific outputs, but it does so decisively in only a subset of fields.

However, it is premature to conclude from these trends that American leadership is on the wane. The US may retain its global lead, not in actual quantity of outputs but in their quality. One approximate measure of quality is to look at how often one nation's research is referenced in the scientific literature. Analysing the extent to which US publications are cited in other papers presents an interesting counterweight to the data on publication volumes. In particular, an analysis of the top 1% of papers by subsequent citation count suggests that even though the US share of total scientific articles in some fields has declined, the influence of US research still remains highly significant. The US accounts for at least a third of the top 1% of cited papers across all fields, with agricultural sciences being the only exception. In fields such as astronomy, all the life sciences and the social sciences, the US still accounts for more than half of the world's most highly cited papers.

By comparison, China accounts for less than a tenth of the top 1% of cited papers across nearly all fields, the main exceptions being engineering and chemistry, in which fields China now accounts respectively for 12% and 11% of the world's top papers by citation count (NSF 2012). One could infer that Americans still seem to publish a disproportionately large number of the world's most important papers. However the US share of highly cited articles declined in every field from the mid-1990s to the late-2000s. While the US continues to hold onto its pre-eminence using this particular measure, it is difficult to see how it can maintain this position indefinitely, especially if its share of global outputs continues to decline.

Economic factors will be important here. The intellectual wealth of a nation is not solely determined by the relative success of its national economy. Cultural factors, geography, migration patterns and the quality of a society's education system are also important; yet there is no denying that the more prosperous a nation, the greater its capacity to excel in science. The strength of the post-war American economy has enabled the US to lead the world in scientific productivity over the past sixty years but, so long as the US continues to contribute a declining share of global economic activity, its share of global science may likewise diminish.

This is best understood as an area of ongoing uncertainty. For the time being, the US continues to provide a considerable proportion of the world's scientific outputs. The US still hosts a disproportionately large number of the best researchers across all fields, at least as determined by their capacity to generate highly cited papers. But the long-term future of US science hangs in the balance. For wealthy nations with sound education systems and a political belief in the value of public investment in science, it is relatively easy to buy scientific infrastructure and to build capability quickly. Ongoing weakness in the American economy will affect the US capacity to invest in research and lead the world across a broad range of fields, and only a resurgence of the American economy in the years ahead will enable the US to maintain its current standing as the leading scientific nation.

2.5 Relative to other nations, the US remains the clear global leader in innovation

Western Pacific nations may draw several interesting conclusions from the data presented above. First, it can be stated unequivocally that the US and China are both nations with excellent prospects. Over recent decades, the decline in innovation performance has been far more marked for Europe than for the US. As a consequence, Europe's global significance as a source of new technologies and ideas is rapidly diminishing. During our current century, and especially in contrast to the reality of the past four hundred years, those nations surrounding the Pacific can expect to play a much greater role in pushing the limits of human ingenuity than their European counterparts. This is worth noting because it underscores the importance of international relationships with both the US and China, these being the two predominant economies in the region.

Second, in forging such relationships it helps to comprehend the technological orientation of both China and the US. For the time being, American society still harbours powerful capabilities across a wide range of technological and scientific domains, while China's strengths seem particularly concentrated around information and communications technologies and within the physical sciences and engineering. Competition, trade and collaboration between Chinese and American organisations is likely to be intense in the latter fields of endeavour, and in these areas, outsiders will need to develop relationships with partners in both countries. In other domains, especially in the life sciences and biotechnology, competition from China is not yet occurring on the same scale. In these areas, outsiders seeking foreign partnerships will likely continue to favour the US.

The third and final point is that broad convergence between China and the US is still a long way off. For those who have seen American innovation as a force for good in the world, and for those who have grown accustomed to a strong and creative economy in the US, the evidence of American decline may seem troubling. But this evidence does not yet support definitive long-term projections about the future. In private-sector innovation, technological invention and scientific discovery, America is still the global leader. Across each of these domains, China is emerging as an important competitor, but it still has a considerable way to go before it can match the US in the size or quality of its innovative activities. In the intervening years, it is conceivable that Americans will respond to the emerging competitive threat posed by China with a future rush of technological ingenuity. As we shall discuss next, American society retains many of the cultural attributes necessary to make this possible.

3. The Value of Liberty

American success in innovation can be attributed to a host of disparate causes. The development of large homogeneous markets, the nature of American political and social institutions, the existence of plentiful natural resources, the impact of the destructive wars in Europe, and the migration of talented and well-educated people from other parts of the world can all be listed as factors that have advantaged the American innovative economy during the twentieth century. Equally important, however, have been a number of cultural characteristics. The can-do spirit, the belief in individual freedom, the ideal of the self-made man, the celebration of entrepreneurship, competition and the consumption culture are attributes that can also be linked to American strength in innovation. Moreover these characteristics seem to endure in American society despite the economic turmoil presented by the financial collapse of 2008 and their persistence should provide grounds for optimism about American innovation in the years ahead.

Innovation is much more than just a technological phenomenon in the US. The desire to innovate appears to be a fundamental aspect of American society. Over recent times, the US has been a leader not only in technological or scientific innovation, but also in business-model innovation and in the development and dissemination of cultural goods. American commercial practices are routinely copied in other parts of the world. American products continue to dominate global sales within the motion picture, television, and music industries. These themes attest not only to the breadth of innovative capacity existing in the US, but also to the ubiquity and resilience within American society of the liberty that enables and encourages experimentation and innovation. These themes ought to provide some pause to those who see American decline as an inevitable corollary of the growth in China's economy.

3.1 American innovation encompasses much more than technology

For many years, the success of US business enterprise has been underpinned not only by technological leadership but also by an extraordinary capacity for business innovation. Business-model innovation has played a pivotal role in the success of America's best-known corporations. Part of the reason organisations like McDonald's, Domino's Pizza, Walt Disney,

Amazon, eBay, Starbucks, Apple and Microsoft have been so successful is that they have been able to identify and then exploit new business models. US corporate history is peppered with examples of organisational innovation, business process innovation, and clever market positioning.

Partly as a consequence of this, US corporations are often highly ranked in global league tables. Even today US firms account for a disproportionately large share of the world's most admired companies, the world's strongest brands and the world's largest companies by market capitalisation and by turnover (Fortune 2012a, Interbrand 2011, FT 2010, DIUS 2010, Fortune 2012b). These league tables reflect the ongoing strength in US business innovation, although the rankings have shifted in curious ways over recent years. For example, US firms have actually been increasing their share of Fortune's most admired companies (at 80% in 2010, up from 50% in 2006), yet their share of global activity by other measures, such as their share of top global brands or their share of largest companies by market capitalisation, has been declining. Perhaps more significantly, the US share of the largest corporations by turnover fell to 28% in 2010 (down from 31% in 2006), a level significantly lower than Europe's 35% share.

On the other hand there is not much evidence that China, which hosts a growing number of firms with very large turnovers, has itself been able to nurture companies with strong brands or companies that are admired globally for their innovative approach to business. By 2012 there were just two Chinese firms on Fortune Magazine's ranking of the world's most admired companies (Fortune 2012a) and in 2011 there were still no Chinese companies on the Interbrand list of the best global brands (Interbrand 2011). For the time being, it would seem that novel and interesting trends in business remain far more likely to originate in the US and to be copied in China than vice versa.

But rankings of leading firms convey only a limited sense of the underlying scope for non-technological innovation in an economy. Perhaps a more objective metric and one that has some bearing on a country's potential for business innovation is the role that knowledge-intensive services play across different societies. Not everybody sees value in this metric. For some commentators, there is a hierarchy of economic virtue in which knowledge-intensive manufacturing is esteemed more than knowledge-intensive commercial services, but this view ought not to temper our analysis. Some sectors are obviously more knowledge-intensive than others, but knowledge-intensive activity in any sector is probably beneficial. In the complex, modern economy, knowledge-intensity will tend to move any industry closer to the frontiers of innovation and on this basis we can use success in knowledge-intensive services as a broad measure of a nation's capacity to innovate in ways that may be dissociated from the production of new technologies.

Commercial knowledge-intensive services can be defined as the business services (including computer and related services), financial services and communications services industries combined. The contributions of these industries globally and regionally can be readily calculated using industry value added measures or, in other words, by calculating net output across these particular industries. An analysis along these lines finds that the US currently accounts for over a third of global knowledge-intensive services activity, slightly more than the European Union, and drastically more than Japan (with less than 10% of global activity) and China (with around 5% of global activity). Furthermore the US share of global commercial knowledge-intensive services has declined only modestly since the mid-1980s, when the US was responsible for over 40% of such services globally (NSF 2010).

This indicates that the US still accounts for a very significant share of global activity in the commercial knowledge-intensive services industries and still accounts for a vastly greater share than China. It is also worth noting that the US has significantly higher proportions of gross domestic product generated within its knowledge-intensive services industries than is true for Europe, Japan or China. The importance of knowledge-intensive services within the US economy and the disproportionately large role of the US economy in these sectors globally may be interpreted as an indication that the US retains a disproportionately large capacity for generating business-model and business-process innovations.

If the US economy seems to enable knowledge-intensive innovation across a broader sectoral base than other economies do, then surely this suggests some underlying features of American society that promote innovation. Another way of looking at this issue is by using the World Bank's knowledge assessment methodology (WB KAM). The World Bank has in recent years developed a "knowledge economy index" intended as a measure of different countries' capacities for generating, adopting and diffusing knowledge. This index aggregates diverse data relating to education, innovation performance, ICT activity, and the economic and regulatory environment. All variables within this process are ranked and normalised on a scale of 0 to 10, with 10 corresponding to the leading country by a given metric. The normalised data is then aggregated to provide a comparative measure of the importance of knowledge in an economy.

Using this methodology, the US emerges easily as the leader among large economic regions: it has a higher knowledge economy index than Europe, Japan or China. But the World Bank's index is not a pure measure of business innovation. It is a composite measure for technological, scientific, and business innovation, and includes measures of science and technology production, which we have dealt with separately. For this reason, it is instructive to analyse a number of more specific metrics independently.

Using the international datasets published by the World Bank (WB KAM), it is easy to rank measures likely to influence a society's capacity for knowledge innovation. Perusing the World Bank datasets one finds data relating to: (i) perceptions about the intensity of local competition as determined by global survey, (ii) the level of tariff and non-tariff barriers in the economy, (iii) the level of employment in the services sector as a percentage of the workforce, (iv) enrolment in tertiary education as a percentage of the age cohort, (v) the quality of management schools as determined by global survey, (vi) the strength of the rule of law, (vii) the availability of venture capital, (viii) the speed with which a business can be set up in an administrative sense, (ix) the cost to register a new business as a percentage of gross national income per capita, (x) the ease of firm-level technology absorption as determined by global survey, (xi) the number of computer users per capita, (xii) the number of internet users per capita and (xiii) the extent of business internet use.

Astonishingly, across every single one of these measures, the US currently comes out demonstrably ahead of Japan, Western Europe, and China—usually in that order. The clear implication is that there remains a strong potential for knowledge-intensive business innovation in the US. Compared with China in particular, American society still looks far more likely to develop novel business ideas. The fascinating implication is that the American economy evidently remains a land of opportunity for innovators across a remarkable diversity of industrial sectors.

3.2 The US remains culturally vibrant

This brings us to a related issue. Throughout the twentieth century, American society has fostered a remarkably vibrant popular culture. Some of the quintessential technologies for creating and disseminating cultural goods during that century were invented within the US. Consider the phonograph and gramophone, the motion picture, the electric guitar, the video game and the Internet. Others were originally invented elsewhere, such as the radio, television, the audiocassette and the compact disc. However, in all cases American society played a decisive role in the development of these technologies, while American-based artists and cultural entrepreneurs consistently led the world in exploiting these technologies for the creation and dissemination of cultural goods.

Arguably the most significant art form of the twentieth century was the motion picture, so let's begin there. The American film industry accounted for around

80% of the world's production of feature films as early as the 1920s (Eyman 1997), a position of dominance that has been underpinned by innumerable innovations, both cultural as well as technological, and that has continued to this day. According to data published in the trade journal, Screen Digest, the US still accounted for around 60% of global production investment in feature films in 2009 and, although its share has been falling over the past decade (from over 70% in 2002), no other region comes close. In 2009, France, Germany, the UK, Spain and Italy combined accounted for less than a quarter of global production investment in feature films, while China accounted for less than 3% of global investment (Screen Australia 2011).

This represents a particularly significant point of distinction between the US and its Asian competitors. As it happens, there are a greater number of films made in India than in the US, but with a negligible capital investment. In China, which has a rapidly growing cinema audience, total production investment also remains modest relative to American expenditures. Even in Japan, where the domestic audience has an established appetite for local stories told in the Japanese language, production financing for feature films relative to the scale of the Japanese economy is very low compared with the situation in the US.

Is this a sign of American creativity? Scale of funding is not always correlated with quality of product in the motion picture industry, but it is often connected with innovation. The American blockbuster has underpinned many of the great innovations in movie making, from the introduction of sound in the 1920s through to today's use of elaborate digital special effects. If it can be sustained, the sheer scale of American investment in feature films will continue to provide American products with significant advantages in the global film market.

What is true for film is also true for popular music. From Latvia to Paraguay, from India to South Korea, American music has made remarkable inroads into popular culture everywhere. For decades American artists have been global artists, achieving high rankings in radio airplay and national sales charts. This is a trade that is rarely reciprocated. With the exception perhaps of the United Kingdom, foreign artists have not done so well in the US as American artists have done abroad.

This asymmetry is consistently illustrated in the music charts, as evidenced by album sales for the US and Europe in 2010 when just two of the top 10 artists selling albums in the US were European, and five of the top 10 artists selling albums in Europe were American. English-speaking musicians accounted for all but three artists across both these lists. Moreover, across both markets almost all of these best-selling albums were in musical genres with American roots. American music is not only exported into other markets; it has shaped the musical tastes of consumers in other markets in profound and lasting ways.

Even in Japan, where consumers have again tended to be patriotic in their music purchasing habits, the trend is similar. Most of the non-Japanese artists featuring in the Japanese charts are American, and it is extremely rare for Japanese artists to break into the US market in a reciprocal way. Furthermore, many Japanese artists seem to find success with Japanese consumers by emulating American musical styles. For the time being, it is very clear that American artists remain the trendsetters for music globally.

While Americans excel in the production of motion pictures and music, things are not quite so clear-cut within another growing creative industry: the electronic games sector. The key issue here is that the longstanding dominance of Nintendo, Sony, and previously Sega, in the production of video game consoles gives the impression that it is the Japanese, not the Americans, who dominate in this area. However, a distinction should be drawn between those firms producing the hardware for playing games, whether consoles, handheld devices, personal computers or mobile phones, and those firms focusing on the development of actual game content.

The US still leads in the latter respect, as is evidenced by aggregating sales data not by hardware provider nor by the region where sales occur, but rather by the countries in which games developers are located. In recent years, global sales of games developed in the US have been consistently twice the sales of games developed in Japan, three times the sales of games developed in the UK, France and Germany combined, and more than four times the sales of games developed in China (Gibson 2008). In other words, although Japanese firms dominate on the hardware side, US games companies continue to account for a disproportionately large share of games development. The US still arguably dominates in gaming software and on the cultural, as opposed to the technological, side of this business.

But this a changing market: the electronic games market in Asia is now larger than that in either North America or Europe, and the market in China is growing very rapidly. In the long run this trend seems likely to create much greater opportunities for Asian development firms than for American firms. Chinese consumers can be expected to have an appetite for Chinese-language products and for products that are sensitive to nuances of Chinese culture. The Chinese may show a strong preference for games developed locally and, in turn, this may reduce the relative importance of American culture within the global gaming industry. The industry is also being affected by the decline of retail gaming and by the rapid growth of online gaming, and of mobile gaming in Japan. This is a very turbulent time for the sector. Unquestionably there is growing competition from Asia and mounting uncertainty about optimal distribution models. But for the time being, it seems that American firms are still the most active creators of electronic games.

The strength of the US position in generating movies, music and games is arguably a function of the size of America's domestic economy. The large domestic market in the US, combined with the size of the English-speaking market worldwide, has afforded significant economies in scale for the production of cultural goods in the US that smaller nations cannot match. With the emergence of a large Chinese middle class, this apparent American advantage seems set to erode over time. Yet for the moment, American products continue to dominate global consumption markets for cultural goods. A diminution in the relative significance of American culture may be coming, but it is not yet upon us.

Furthermore, enormous technological changes compound the future uncertainties. There is an old thesis that the technologies used to disseminate cultural products during the twentieth century created "winner-take-all" markets (Frank 1995). Twentieth century technology meant that the best American artists could capture revenue from a very high proportion of American consumers. The returns to American artists could be very high indeed; a situation that seems to have fostered considerable scale of production as well as competition and innovation across a number of creative industries.

Today's dissemination technologies, by contrast, seem to be creating fragmented markets or "long-tail" markets (Anderson 2006). In this scenario, the advantages of scale may be diminishing, although this is not yet clear. Some of the business processes that worked in the past are now starting to fail. Bookstores and main street music stores have been closing. Television audiences have been shrinking. Internet participation has led to new models for consuming, sharing and even creating cultural goods. Moreover, as the recording companies and newspapers have shown, in the new technological environment incumbency may prove a weakness rather than a source of strength.

The magnitude of this challenge has been especially acute for the American music industry. Over the first decade of the twenty-first century, sales of compact discs plummeted within the US domestic market, and this decline was nowhere near being matched by growth in digital sales. Astonishingly, in 2009 the revenues from music sales within the US were less than half their 1999 peak and were actually lower in real terms than in the 1970s (RIAA 2011). This is a time of tremendous challenge, and not just for this particular sector. The extent to which Internet technology will disrupt distribution models for other cultural goods is only beginning to become apparent. But does this signal the end of American dominance in the creation of new music or other new cultural products globally?

In answering this question, it is critical to recognise that these challenges exist not only for American firms—they are global. The big question is where people are most likely to invent the new distribution models that will reach the greatest number of consumers and create the most value. The answer, judging not least from the recent international success of unorthodox US retailers like Amazon, eBay, iTunes and Spotify, is that the US will likely emerge again as the dominant force in the dissemination of culture, and hence it will likely remain the dominant producer too.

Much depends upon the vibrancy and creativity of the Chinese. Cultural products for mass consumption are increasingly digital in nature and distributed via Internet portals. Moreover, following an important inflection that occurred around 2007, there are now more Internet users in China than in the US (WB 2011). This represents a remarkable potential market for Chinese artists and cultural entrepreneurs and ought to stimulate the growth of very significant indigenous cultural industries. However, the scale of these industries and the relevance of their products to consumers in other parts of the world will be determined by factors other than pure demographics.

The creation of cultural goods requires a particular sort of creativity; artistic creativity is quite distinct from technical or technological creativity. The creation of *popular* cultural goods in turn requires an ability to marry this artistic creativity with an understanding of consumer desire. If Chinese society can foster individual self-expression and a consumerist culture on a scale to rival the US, then there is reason to imagine that China's cultural industries will eventually rival those in the US. However, in the absence of these trends it is difficult to see any other society matching American dominance in the creation of cultural goods for many decades.

3.3 The US possesses a number of social and cultural advantages

The causes of the American propensity for innovation are complex. The size of the American domestic market, the migration of scientists to the US before and after the Second World War, and the lack of an entrenched class structure were all circumstances that favoured the US in the twentieth century. Important too were the American institutions of governance: the rule of law and a federal system of government that historically created checks upon the intervention of government in economic life. Over most of the twentieth century, the machinery of government in the US proved less inclined to impede innovative businesses than was true in many other parts of the world.

However, the sheer breadth of American innovation suggests that cultural forces are also at play. It is hard to imagine a society as vibrant, as creative, and as dynamic as the US, which didn't also cultivate innovation through its underlying values. The can-do spirit, a belief in individualism, the ideal of the self-made man, the cultural acceptance of mobility within the population, and the celebration of entrepreneurship are clichés of American life that can be linked to American strength in innovation (Barlow 2008). Salient too is the American middle-class ability to see inquisitiveness and acquisitiveness as compatible, the American veneration of consumption, and the deep-seated American belief in the value of liberty. For those who remain sceptical about America's capacity to recover from recent economic events and from the debilitating levels of government debt currently being held in the US, these cultural attributes should be regarded as important. So long as American society nourishes cultural values that celebrate innovative and entrepreneurial behaviours, it will arguably retain a significant capacity to continue innovating independent of broader economic or political frameworks.

It is interesting to consider the evidence that American society regards inquisitiveness and acquisitiveness as both desirable and compatible. These two qualities do not always associate. There are plenty of communities that celebrate curiosity while denigrating the urge to make money. This is a common position in many intellectual communities, especially in academic institutions. There is also the countervailing archetype: the entrepreneur very interested in making money, but affecting no interest in knowledge for its own sake. In the US there is evidence that this disconnection is less common than is true elsewhere, for inquisitiveness and acquisitiveness are more often associated in the US than is true within other societies.

That the US is an acquisitive society is evident. It is the largest economy in the world, and it has one of the highest levels of gross domestic product per capita. By and large, Americans are not embarrassed by money. Wealth and its ostentatious consumption confer status in the US. American society places a great deal of importance upon wealth-accumulation and consumption. Yet the US is also the nation that invests the most in knowledge. The OECD defines investment in knowledge as investment in R&D plus software plus higher education. International data along these lines, normalised against gross domestic product, clearly demonstrate the distinctiveness of the US position. As a share of its economy the US invests more in knowledge than Japan and nearly twice as much as Europe (OECD Scoreboard). Unfortunately similar data is not available on China, although its level of investment would likely be more modest still.

One of the unusual features of the American investment in knowledge is the scale of the American investment in higher education. This investment has bought the American universities an extraordinary level of global dominance. Even today, over half of the top 100 universities in the Shanghai Jiao Tong ranking of world universities are American institutions (SJTU 2012). This is a proportion obviously well beyond the US's share of the global economy, and it should be noted here that the American love affair with higher education is not a recent phenomenon. There is a tendency to see the global dominance of US universities during the late twentieth century as a corollary simply of the nation's economic success. But the history of intellectual endeavour in the US is a remarkably long one: at the time of the American revolution in 1776, there were already nine universities in the 13 British colonies of North America, supporting a population of only 2.5 million people (Maddison 2006).

American universities also prove an interesting case study because they show a peculiar capacity for linking intellectual pursuits with commercial activity. In 2010 American universities accounted for 16 of the top 20 patenting academic institutions worldwide, as measured by international patent applications through the PCT process, and for 30 of the top 50 patenting academic institutions (WIPO 2011). The dominance of American institutions by these measures, and the weakness especially of European institutions, is quite at odds with the distribution patterns of traditional scientific outputs such as scientific publications.

The implication here is either (a) that American research is superior to research in other places, or (b) that American universities are simply more comfortable about trying to profit from their research than is true in other parts of the world. Both of these explanations are important, but the pivotal observation is that American universities are acquisitive as well as inquisitive institutions. By global standards, universities in the US illustrate a peculiar capacity to balance two values that are often regarded as incompatible.

Now the level of American investment in knowledge, and especially in higher education, can seem surprising on account of other competing prejudices that exist about American society. In surveys of general knowledge, US citizens do not excel relative to the citizens of other nations. Likewise in global assessments of school-level education in mathematics and science, American children do not stand out relative to other nations. Indeed there is growing evidence that a significant proportion of American school children are either poorly taught or lack the interest to study science and mathematics seriously (NSF 2010 and OECD PISA). Apparently not all Americans possess the desire to develop and express their own intellectual curiosity.

But even if inquisitiveness appears not to be a prevailing value for every American, at the individual level, nonetheless a surprising number do see the value of scientific enquiry for their society as a whole. The

National Science Foundation has published the results of several surveys of public attitudes towards science in the US and around the world, revealing the following results:

- Americans support investment in knowledge without demonstrable, near-term benefit. For over twenty years, ~80% of Americans surveyed have said they believe that the federal government should fund basic scientific research (NSF 2010).
- A very high proportion of Americans see science as a force for good. In 2008, ~70% of Americans surveyed agreed that "the benefits of scientific research outweighed the harmful results", compared with ~60% of Chinese, ~50% of Europeans, and ~40% of Japanese (NSF 2010).
- Americans see science as pervasive and highly relevant to their lives. Only 14% of Americans surveyed in 2004 agreed with the statement "it is not important for me to know about science in my daily life" compared with an astonishing 37% of Europeans surveyed in 2005 (NSF 2010).

American attitudes to scientific enquiry and to the development of new technologies are resolutely optimistic and show persistent community support. The distinctions with Europe in this respect are especially striking. Indeed, judging from international surveys like these and from attitudes to novel and controversial technologies such as genetically modified crops, the US is still a global outlier, though it is also worth noting that China is now more avant-garde, and more like the US in these respects than is Europe.

This is a very important point to make in evaluating the future prospects for innovation in the US. Community support for science, innovation and technological change is an important attribute of American society. It underpins US political support for research investment. It engenders openness to ideas and to change—a hallmark of all great innovating societies. Europe during the Renaissance, Britain during the Industrial Revolution, Germany in the late nineteenth century, and Japan following the Second World War: all these offer excellent examples of this connection (see, for example, Mokyr 1990). At a deeper level though, the American faith in science and technology also increases the likelihood that American markets will continue to reward American entrepreneurs.

Inquisitiveness is also important for innovative societies where it is able to associate with consumption behaviours. It is worth recognising that the US has long stood out in global terms not just for the scale of its consumer markets, but also for the inquisitiveness of its consumers. Customer needs and values have played a pivotal role in shaping American innovation. Users were responsible for many of the major technological innovations developed across a range of American industries throughout the twentieth century (Hippel 1998, Hippel 2005), and the US remains distinctive for its large numbers of venturesome consumers who value novelty and have an appetite both for buying and trying new technologies (Bhidé 2008). This should be seen as an enduring cultural advantage for the US, for innovating firms and entrepreneurs are more likely to find opportunities in an environment that naturally desires their outputs than in one where novelty is regarded with suspicion or met with inertia.

There is an interesting contrast to be drawn with China in this respect. China does have a rapidly growing consumer market, and various indicators suggest that Chinese consumers are proving venturesome, especially in relation to goods that signal status and wealth. But the Chinese model of economic development, focussing on exports while constraining domestic consumption, can only have acted as a check on the role of Chinese consumers in driving domestic innovation. In this context, it is not surprising that Americans still constitute a significant proportion of customers for many of China's most innovative businesses.

This brings us to a critical issue. A key determinant of American innovation has been the liberty in which American citizens are able to conduct their lives. Americans possess remarkable freedoms, not just as citizens but also as producers and consumers. It is up to every American to define his or her own route to the good life. American culture values individual liberty and individual freedom of choice. As a consequence, innovation in the US has traditionally been an emergent phenomenon rather than a directed phenomenon; it has been the result of a myriad of individual choices made within competitive markets rather than of nationalistic planning and enlightened government. Back in the early 1920s, Frederick Jackson Turner captured this concept when he stated that the American frontier was conquered "by the ideal of the self-made man, rather than by the ideal of industrial nationalism" (Turner 1921). Perhaps this model is less applicable to the US today than it once was. At the frontiers of technology and commerce, one can point to a growing appetite for government intervention in the automobile sector, financial services, healthcare and energy markets. Nonetheless, this sentiment is still strong in the American psyche.

This should be held up as a reason for optimism about America's future. Liberty stimulates innovation. Liberty permits the neglect of traditions, dogmas and social hierarchies. It forces producers to makes things that people genuinely want, and to dream up new products that people never previously imagined they needed. It also forces producers to compete for resources and to find ways to reduce the costs of their products.

A free society favours consumers and innovation ahead of political interests, and for this reason one should be extremely cautious about writing off the American innovation machine just yet.

3.4 Other nations will still find much to emulate in the US

Admittedly, for the first time in living memory the US is experiencing serious erosion of its global dominance in innovation. Relative to other nations, the US share of global innovation is diminishing, and given the economic expansion and the growing sophistication of the developing world, this is a change that looks increasingly inexorable. Yet one should not exaggerate the significance of this trend. American society retains considerable resilience. As we have seen, the US remains by far the leading innovative nation. By most metrics, the scale of innovative activity in the US still dwarfs that in other nations, including China. The US is also generally more intensive in its reliance upon science, technology and innovation than other societies. At the same time, American values are still firmly conducive to innovation and to the development of new technologies and new ideas. This is true in a way that cannot be said of some other parts of the developed world.

There are a number of implications here for people in other nations who may be trying to come to terms with the shifting geographic distribution of innovative activity across the Pacific. First, it should be observed that business model innovations, as opposed to technological innovations, remain much more likely to emerge from the US than any other nation. Business leaders and policy makers in other Western Pacific nations should recognise that innovations, and most particularly those within the services sectors, remain more likely to be produced by American firms than Chinese ones.

Second, it is difficult to avoid the following observation about cultural creativity. People involved in the creation of mass-market cultural goods across many parts of the world will presumably find plenty of new opportunities in China over the coming years and decades. In China itself, the growth of the domestic market for cultural goods will unquestionably stimulate local content producers. However, it seems likely that the major jumps in innovation and creativity in the cultural space will continue to occur in the US. The overall Chinese market for cultural goods will undoubtedly exceed that of the US in time, but the US looks to remain the more innovative producer of cultural products for the foreseeable future.

This brings us to our final observation. The values that have underpinned American innovation are different from the values that are being used to stimulate a transformation in the Chinese innovation system.

This is an issue that we will deal with more fully in subsequent chapters, but let us note a few interesting implications: outsiders will often need to adopt different approaches when connecting with prospective partners in the US and in China, the distinctive nature of the American value system implies versatility and resilience in uncertain times, and if the US can only resolve its current political problems (especially that of government debt) without undermining these values, then the long-term prospects for American innovation should still be very positive. This is not the moment for Western Pacific countries to disconnect from the US.

4. The Dragon

Growing impressions of Chinese economic ascendency have clearly influenced perceptions of decline in the US. But explosive as its transformation has been over recent decades, the Chinese economy still has a long way to go before it will match the US economy in terms of productivity, technological sophistication and business creativity. The remarkable growth in Chinese information and communications technology manufacturing is certainly a rapidly emerging strength. China's success in this area is a significant development, not least since every new factory is a potential training ground for future entrepreneurs and inventors. Although the rise of Chinese manufacturing does not yet imply a wholesale loss of American leadership in innovation, it does foreshadow that possibility.

But there is a world of difference between possibility and certainty. Most discussions about the relative competitive positions of China and the US are really discussions about the future or, more precisely, about different peoples' projections of the future. Yet much of the current bullish speculation about China's future is based purely upon (a) what has happened within the Chinese economy over the past thirty years, and (b) perceptions about the sheer size of the Chinese population and what this means for China's innovative potential. In our view, it is not inevitable that this bigger and more powerful economy will also produce an explosion in Chinese technological creativity to rival that of America. Our goal is to articulate a more nuanced story.

China faces a number of conflicting forces. On one hand, China does have a remarkable demographic advantage. According to official statistics, it already hosts more industrial researchers than either Japan or the European Union and, even though the number of Chinese aged between 20 and 24 years has peaked, China still has capacity to continue growing its educated population. On the other hand, the quality of intellectual property currently being created in China should raise questions about China's future as a technological and creative power. Also at issue is the fact that China is not a homogeneous entity. Some regions are vastly more technologically sophisticated and innovative than others. Unless China is able to replicate nationally what has happened in a Special Economic Zone like Shenzen, national projections based upon the advantages anticipated from China's scale may ultimately prove misleading.

4.1 China has an important demographic advantage

In the long run, by virtue of its scale alone, China should have an excellent prospect of evolving into a powerhouse of innovation. As we have discussed, larger economies create more opportunities for competition than smaller economies. Larger economies typically have disproportionately larger scope for making investments in risky, knowledge-intensive ventures than smaller economies. All other things being equal, larger societies also have a larger pool of human talent to draw upon.

This latter dimension is especially critical for China. The scale of its labour force represents an important aspect of the country's comparative advantage, and is a common cause of optimism about China's innovation potential. China has a population of 1.3 billion, compared with just over 300 million in the US (WB 2011). The importance of this disparity should not be overemphasised. There are also a billion people in Africa and few commentators in the West anticipate a near-term explosion of innovation on that continent. China's demographic advantage is that its society has been able to mobilise the productivity of an increasing proportion of its massive population through education and rapid urbanisation. It is the scale of China's urban, educated population, not the scale of its population as a whole, which will ultimately have the significant ramifications for China's economy and its levels of innovation.

China's urbanisation has been very well documented. The number of Chinese citizens living in cities of more than 1 million people has exceeded that of the US since 1991. Two decades later, China has over 230 million citizens living in cities of over 1 million people, compared with fewer than 140 million people in the US (WB 2011). The scale and density of China's urban population is significant not just for its raw economic consequences, but also because there appear to be strong connections between city life and creativity (Florida 2005).

Moreover, the urbanisation of China's population is by no means complete. Even now, around half of China's population still live in rural areas, compared with less than a fifth of the population in the US, and less than 20% of China's population lives in cities of over 1 million people, compared with over 40% in the US and Japan, and around 60% in Australia (WB 2011). The continuing movement of people from rural environments to cities is likely to increase the opportunities available to individual Chinese with respect to education, work and the development of skills.

This increasing opportunity is manifest in the growing educational qualifications of the Chinese workforce and the rising number of researchers in the Chinese economy. Between 2000 and 2008, the number of students graduating with first degrees in China quadrupled. As a consequence, Chinese universities now graduate nearly 2.3 million students a year. This includes 300,000 students with an undergraduate degree in science and over 700,000 with an undergraduate degree in engineering (NSF 2012). To give a sense of scale, China now graduates 40% more first-degree students annually than the US, including over 60% more scientists and an eye-raising ten times as many engineers.

The recent and rapid transition in its higher education system clearly has profound consequences for China's innovative potential. Moreover, there is considerable capacity for these numbers keep growing. If we include graduates from tertiary colleges as well as universities, then the number of Chinese students graduating from higher education institutions actually exceeded 7 million in 2010 (Yearbook 2011). Of course one can question the quality of education received by all these graduates compared with that received by students in Western institutions; despite its expanding domestic higher education system, more students still leave China to study abroad than is true for any other country. In 2009 there were still over 100,000 Chinese students enrolled in American universities (Burrelli 2010). The raw numbers do tell us something important, however. They reflect a society that values education, a society in which large numbers of people are finding the means to enhance their skills formally and increase their knowledge.

At more advanced levels of study, a similar picture emerges. The number of doctoral students graduating from Chinese universities has also grown dramatically over recent decades. In the early 1990s around 2,000 PhDs graduated annually in China, a figure that had risen to nearly 50,000 by 2010 (NSF 2012 and Yearbook 2011). As a consequence, Chinese universities now graduate considerably more PhDs than Japanese universities. There is still a little way to go in order to match the number of PhDs awarded annually in Europe (over 100,000 in 2008) or in the US (over 60,000), but the difference is rapidly narrowing.

Even more elucidating is the picture that emerges if one examines graduation rates by discipline. Chinese institutions are now graduating as many PhDs in engineering and the sciences as American institutions. In both China and the US in 2008, around a quarter of PhD graduates were in the sciences, but more than a third of Chinese PhD graduates were engineers compared with only 13% of American PhD graduates (NSF 2010). Figures like these naturally raise concerns about US technological competitiveness, although the benefits of a PhD education may be channelled more into building up China's public sector and higher education capacity than into industry.

This brings us to one very tangible effect associated with the growth in PhD programs at Chinese universities: the elevation in the status of Chinese universities in international league tables. Between 1998 and 2010 the number of higher education institutions in China more than doubled (from 1022 to 2358), and by 2010 around half of these institutions (1112) were universities with full undergraduate courses, around half of which again offered postgraduate programs (Yearbook 2011). What's more, a small but growing number of these institutions are achieving international visibility.

According to one metrics-based ranking system of research performance, mainland China now has 4 universities ranked in the top 200 and 28 universities ranked in the top 500 worldwide (SJTU 2012). In absolute terms, these are still fairly modest figures. In this particular ranking system, the US has more universities in the top 40 globally than China has in the top 500, and the US accounted for 85 of the top 200 universities. On the other hand, China now has more universities in the top 500 than Australia, Canada or Japan. More importantly, China has momentum on its side. When this particular ranking system was started in 2003, China had only 9 universities in the top 500 and none in the top 200. Given the growth in research-trained graduates and the growing investment in public research and development, in coming years one should expect the ranking of Chinese institutions to climb steadily.

Such developments are no doubt of prime importance. No nation can aspire to lead the global economy of ideas without outstanding educational institutions. The production of vast numbers of engineers and PhDs in China has been consistent with another even more significant trend: alongside its boom in higher education and in its economy, China has experienced remarkable growth in the number of its researchers—yet another measure of its potential as a centre of new discoveries, ideas and innovations.

From 2000 to 2010 the number of researchers in China almost doubled to reach around 1.2 million (OECD MSTI). This is similar to the number of researchers in the US (1.4 million in 2007) and in the European Union (1.4 million in 2010) and dwarfs the number of researchers in Japan (fewer than 700,000). Many of these researchers will be engineers rather than PhD graduates; many will focus on development rather than research, and the average productivity of these researchers may be low relative to researchers in developed countries. Yet even with these caveats, the sheer scale of the research workforce in China represents a significant advance.

It is important to note that a growing proportion of these Chinese researchers are operating in industry, rather than within the public sector. In the early 1990s, nearly three quarters of China's research labour force was based in the public sector, a proportion similar to that in Australia. By contrast around 60% of China's researchers are based in industry today. Indeed, this proportion is approaching that found in the US. Around 80% of all American researchers work in industry and in Europe only around 50% of researchers work in industry; these two proportions have been fairly stable over the past two decades (OECD MSTI).

To gain some perspective on this transition, it should be recognised that in the early 1990s the vast majority of Chinese researchers worked within government-controlled entities: either in government research institutes or in state-owned enterprises. Over the intervening two decades, many of these government research institutes have been converted to non-profit research institutes with responsibility for their own management and independence from government (Hu 2008). Even state-owned enterprises account for a diminishing share of the industrial research and development personnel in China (Yearbook 2011).

The growing number of business-sector researchers in China is a huge phenomenon. China is now second only to the US in the number of its business enterprise researchers. Indeed there are now more researchers working in businesses in China than there are in the European Union or in Japan and South Korea combined (OECD MSTI). This is an extraordinary and potentially disruptive development for the global economy.

Furthermore, the remarkable growth in China's educated workforce seems likely to continue. On one hand, China does face a curious demographic challenge in the years ahead. Owing to repressive family planning policies introduced in 1979, the number of Chinese aged between 20 and 24 years (the age at which most people attend university or college) has already peaked. In stark contrast to the situation in India, the numbers in this particular age group are set to decline dramatically over the next forty years (NSF 2010). This could suggest a slowing of opportunities for China but, on the other hand, there are two factors that may limit the impact this trend. First, it should be recognised that even in 2050 the number of Chinese in this age bracket will be about four times as large as that in the US. Second, for the foreseeable future it is likely that this demographic dwindling can be counterbalanced by China's ongoing urbanisation. With half of China's population still based in rural areas and with less than 20% of China's population living in cities of more than a million people (WB 2011), clearly there is still a great mass of untapped human capital in China. In this respect, China's long-term prospects seem very strong.

4.2 Questions remain about the quality of China's intellectual property

The number of university graduates and researchers in China is certainly breathtaking. But what are all these people likely to achieve in practice? Judging the capacities of those trained and working in China today and the politicised environment in which many of them must operate, one cannot help but feel ambivalent about China's long-term creative and technological prospects. On the one hand, China's newly educated workforce has clearly helped to reinvolve China in the global production of knowledge, and the Chinese are now rapidly increasing the rate at which they are creating new intellectual property. On the other hand, ongoing political interference is undermining the quality of China's public research system and challenging questions remain about the success of Chinese efforts to create globally valuable intellectual property.

As we saw in our analysis of the US, China has rapidly grown its share of world scientific outputs in recent years, particularly in the physical sciences. In its scale of total publications, China overtook France in 2004, Germany and the UK in 2006, and Japan in 2007. Measured by scientific papers, as we have already discussed, China is now the second most productive nation, producing nearly 10% of the global total in 2009. China may have already eclipsed the US in the volume of its physics and chemistry articles.

Yet scientific productivity does not necessarily ensure technological or innovative superiority. In recent years, Europe has equalled US production of scientific articles in the life sciences, yet it was the US not Europe that nurtured the more vibrant biotechnology industry. Recently Europe has out-produced the US in physics publications, but the US continues to produce the greater share of international information and communications technology innovations.

There is also an underlying question about the quality of Chinese research. Even within China, researchers have been highly critical of the capacity of the Chinese public funding system to channel funds to those scientists best qualified to use them. Two eminent life scientists from universities in Beijing recently wrote that China's public research culture "wastes resources, corrupts the spirit and stymies innovation." They observed that funding processes were excessively political rather than merit-based. "To obtain major grants in China, it is an open secret that doing good research is not as important as schmoozing with powerful bureaucrats and their favourite experts," they wrote in the leading journal Science (Shi 2010).

If these claims are true, then the present scientific culture in China limits this nation's potential. But such a culture can change with time. A great number of Chinese scientists have been trained in the US and are accustomed to operating in a highly competitive and meritocratic environment. The scale of activity and the growing scale of outputs in China provide a solid platform from which to build better future performance. And yet one should take care not to jump to conclusions about the strength of China's scientific and technological capability based solely upon these publication numbers.

A more realistic measure of commercial innovative capacity may be afforded by patent data. As already discussed, patents are an imperfect indicator and their value is difficult to quantify at a national level, but they can provide a better indication of commercially valuable intellectual property than that suggested by quantity of scientific publications. This is especially true in the areas of manufacturing and trade where the Chinese economy has expanded capacity over recent years.

As we have seen, while China has a strong presence in the scientific literature, its share of international patents is less impressive, although its performance is changing quickly. Despite recent growth, China still accounts for a moderate share of Patent Cooperation Treaty (PCT) applications made to the World Intellectual Property Organisation. In 2010, over 27% of PCT applications originated from the US, compared with 7.5% from China (WIPO 2011). But China's share of triadic patent families (i.e. patent families registered at the US, European and Japanese patent offices and sharing one or more priorities) is significantly lower than this. In 2010 Chinese inventors were named on just 875 triadic patent families, compared with around 14,000 for American inventors, over 15,000 for European inventors, and over 15,000 for Japanese inventors (OECD MSTI).

There are also questions about the beneficiaries of current Chinese inventions. Evidence suggests that a significant proportion of the international patents granted with a Chinese inventor end up benefiting non-Chinese firms. A recent analysis identified the top ten firms ranked by number of patents granted at the US Patent and Trademark Office (USPTO) in 2006 and having at least one inventor with a mainland China address. Only three companies on this list were Chinese-owned (Branstetter 2010), the rest being Taiwanese, American, and Japanese:

- Hon Hai / Foxconn (Taiwan)
- Microsoft Corporation (US)
- Inventec Corporation (Taiwan)
- China Petrochemical (China)
- SAE Magnetics (Japan)
- China Petroleum and Chemical Company (China)
- Huawei Technologies (China)
- IBM (US)
- Winbond Electronics (Taiwan)
- Intel (US)
- United Microelectronics (Taiwan)
- Proctor and Gamble (US)

China's relatively low levels of international patenting activity may reflect limitations in current Chinese innovation. It is tempting to draw such a conclusion, especially if one contrasts the scale of international patenting activity with the scale of the Chinese economy and the apparent growing presence of Chinese manufactured goods in global high-technology exports. But the reality is more complex. For example, if one looks at China's international patenting activity through the PCT process, while the volume remains moderate, the growth has been astonishing. China's PCT patent filings in 1998 were equivalent to 0.5% of developed world filings and 16% of developing world filings. A decade later, China accounted for 5% of developed world filings and for 54% of developing world filings (WIPO 2010), and these proportions have continued to grow. Based on these trends, it's conceivable that China's share of PCT patent filings will exceed those of Germany, the leading nation in Europe, within a decade. Chinese applicants already account for more PCT applications than France or the UK.

This seems to suggest a shift in China's ability to develop intellectual property. However these data are only suggestive. It is impossible to assess the quality or value of these patent applications. It is also possible that Chinese firms are simply opting to use the PCT process more frequently than their counterparts in European nations, where it may be more common to apply for patents directly through national patenting offices.

To a certain extent, it is possible to test this hypothesis by tracing the recent trend in the number of patents granted directly by the USPTO, analysed according to inventors' countries of residence. Data for American inventors must be excluded from such an analysis, as there is a strong national bias in evaluating statistics from any national patenting office: inventors tend to protect their intellectual property most enthusiastically in their local markets. For example, US applicants accounted for half of all patents granted by the USPTO in 2010 (NSF 2012). One is thus restricted to comparing China's intellectual property with that of nations outside the US. This noted, such comparisons are worth making because the trends observed from the USPTO are startling and quite different from the trends that we have described from PCT data. The current evidence is that Chinese inventors still account for only a fraction of the US patents granted to Japanese, German or South Korean inventors (NSF 2012). It would seem that Chinese inventors have not yet created a strong intellectual property position directly in the US market, which is still the world's largest market for new technologies.

This is not to say that such a position could not be quickly established and in this respect it may be that the PCT filings data are a leading indicator. It is also worth remembering just how quickly inventors from other Asian countries have historically gained share of USPTO patenting activity. Interestingly, Chinese inventors' share of US patents granted in 2010 was equivalent South Korean inventors' share of US patents granted back in 1998. Today, South Korean inventors are responsible for nearly as many USPTO patents as German inventors and for more than twice as many US patents as French or British inventors. Should China now follow a similar trajectory to South Korea (and it is currently growing at three times South Korea's rate of growth in the 1990s), one would expect China to eclipse France and the UK by share of US patents within only a few years. In other words, it would be premature to judge China's future prospects exclusively according to its current USPTO patent portfolio.

A massive recent expansion in domestic Chinese patenting adds another dimension to our analysis. Over a long period, China has had a very weak intellectual property system. This reflected a communist suspicion of property rights in general and a view that the benefits of research should be exploited as public goods not private property. It was also a natural strategy for a nation that perceived its greater advantage lay in accessing other peoples' intellectual property rather than in protecting its own. Evidence suggests that this is now changing. Over the past decade, there has been huge growth (a more than sixfold increase over the decade to 2010) in the numbers of applications to the Chinese Patent Office. The scale of this growth relative to other patent offices is illustrated by the fact that the Chinese Patent Office now processes more applications annually than the Japanese Patent Office, and well over twice the number of applications processed annually by the European Patent Office (WIPO 2011).

Most of this growth in activity within the Chinese Patent Office can be attributed to a surge in domestic (as opposed to foreign) applications. This rise in applications is a consequence of several effects including the strengthening of intellectual property law and rising R&D investment intensity in the Chinese economy, a surge in foreign direct investment associated with technologically sophisticated industries, and the impetus provided by competition with foreign firms (Hu 2009). These explanations seem to suggest at the very least an emerging understanding of the benefits of intellectual property in China, although significant questions remain concerning the quality of many of these applications. The vast majority of Chinese domestic patent applications made by Chinese applicants have historically been for utility patents (which are not assessed in the Chinese system for novelty and inventive step) as opposed to inventive patents (which are). This leads to the view that Chinese technological innovation is likely to be incremental rather than transformative in nature (Hu 2009).

Such an impression is confirmed by the failure of many domestic patent applications processed by the Chinese Patent Office. The success rate for foreign applicants (i.e. the extent to which applications lead to grants of patents) is much higher for foreign applicants than for domestic applicants.

Interestingly, these same data show that Chinese inventors are applying for patents within China far more often than outside it. Fewer than 5% of all patent applications made by Chinese applicants in 2010 were made to patent offices outside China. Contrast this with the situation in South Korea where 26% of patent applications were made abroad, Japan where 37% of patent applications were made abroad, and the US where 42% of patent applications were made abroad (WIPO 2011). Given that the most valuable intellectual property is usually worth protecting in more than one market, this further supports the notion that Chinese patents are generally of lower quality than is true in leading nations.

It would seem that while China is rapidly growing its patenting activity, it still has a considerable way to go before it can match leading developed countries both in the quality and international orientation of its intellectual property. Hence, caution is recommended when extrapolating directly from the growing scale of China's educated population in order to draw conclusions about China's current capacity for creating globally valuable intellectual property.

4.3 Chinese innovation is clustered along the coast

An additional complication is that prospects for technological advancement in China are not uniform across the country. When considering the future implications of China's recent economic development and the potential implied by its vast population, it must be remembered that China is not a homogeneous entity. The country is immense and encompasses considerable regional variation. Evidently, it is not China in its totality that is emerging as an innovative power, but a subset of its provinces. Official data on R&D spending published annually by the Chinese Government makes this clear. Today, just ten eastern coastal provinces (extending from Liaoning in the north down to Guangdong in the south) account for nearly three quarters of China's business R&D activity. These same regions encompass just 40% of the population and roughly 60% of China's gross domestic product (Yearbook 2011). In other words, relative to population and economic activity, China's industrial R&D activity is concentrated along the coast.

Even within this coastal region there is considerable clustering. 60% of China's business R&D activity occurs in just six administrative divisions, accounting for 30% of the national population and less than half of China's gross domestic product. These administrative divisions are Guangdong in the south, Shandong, Jiangsu, Shanghai, and Zhejiang in the east, and Liaoning in the north (Yearbook 2011). There is also a similar coastal concentration in public sector research, although it has a much greater focus around Beijing and Shanghai.

The importance of the southern coastal region of Guangdong in China's innovative capacity may have longstanding roots. It has been argued that, within this province, entrepreneurship and a commercial instinct are strong and ancient cultural traits (Rawski 2011). It's not all that surprising that the main centres for commercial R&D are based along China's seaboard: accessibility to the rest of the world enables the trade of goods and movement of people that are so critical for stimulating innovation. (The same phenomenon can be observed in other nations—not least in the US.)

Given the extent to which R&D activity is clustered in a minority of Chinese provinces, it is fascinating to compare the innovation of specific Chinese regions with other nations. One simple way of doing this is to contrast the levels of industrial R&D spending in the leading administrative divisions in China with that in leading European nations, Asian nations, and American states. Comparisons along these lines show that, by the scale of their industrial R&D activity, the leading regions in China can now compete directly with European nations and with several US states.

To put things in perspective, reported business R&D spending in Guangdong (normalised for purchasing power parity) now occurs on a greater scale than in any US state except California and is approaching the level of spending in the UK. In both Shandong and Jiangsu business R&D expenditures are close to those of New Jersey and exceed those of Taiwan, Texas, Australia, Canada and Italy. There is also as much business R&D spending in Zhejiang as in Illinois or Sweden. Furthermore, businesses in Shanghai report R&D expenditures greater than those in Israel, the Netherlands or Finland (OECD MSTI, NSF 2012, and Yearbook 2011). These data are not normalised for population or for scale of local economic activity. Business R&D activity in Shanghai amounted to around $340 per person in 2010 compared with around $1000 per person in Finland or Israel. Business R&D spending in Guangdong and Jiangsu was around $200 and $230 per person respectively in 2010, compared with $1,800 per person in California, and over $2,000 per person in New Jersey, Massachusetts and Connecticut in 2008 (NSF 2012, OECD MSTI, Yearbook 2011). However the distinctions are not so great in every case. Business R&D spending in Jiangsu is now greater than that of Italy and Spain both in absolute terms, and in the level of spending per capita. This is perhaps an unfair comparison as Italy and Spain are among Europe's laggards by the latter measure, but it does reinforce the impression of growing innovation performance in some Chinese regions. The low relative intensity of even the leading Chinese clusters also suggests that there is considerable room for these regions to continue expanding their business R&D investment as the Chinese economy grows.

The concentration of Chinese business innovation within a small number of regions is consistent with the historical experience in Europe and the US. Innovative activity naturally tends to cluster geographically. In China's case, though, there is not yet a strong link between the R&D investment in these clusters and international high-technology patenting activity. As we saw earlier, one area of advanced technology in which China is focused and where China appears to be building an international presence is in information and communications technologies. The regions in China responsible for the largest number of PCT patent applications relating to this technological domain are Guangdong, Beijing, Shanghai, Zhejiang and Jiangsu (OECD PD). These were all listed among China's leading regions of industrial R&D investment. But only one of these regions shows up as a globally significant generator of patent applications: Guangdong.

The OECD routinely analyses global clusters by number of PCT applications in information and communications technologies. In recent years these analyses make it apparent that Shenzhen in Guangdong has emerged as a globally important source of invention. Remarkably, after Tokyo and Silicon Valley, Guangdong is now the world's third most prolific source of PCT patent applications relating to information and communications technology (OECD PD).

The same analysis shows that other Chinese centres active in commercial R&D are not establishing similar visibility and are nowhere near as productive in generating intellectual property within this domain. It is interesting to note that in 2009 there were more PCT applications relating to information and communications technologies with Sydney- or Melbourne-based inventors than there were with inventors based in Zhejiang, Jiangsu, or Shandong combined.

This begs a question about the focus of China's innovation clusters outside of Guangdong. A similar analysis of patenting activity in biotechnology reveals only very modest Chinese activity. The leading centres for biotechnology patenting across China in 2009 were Beijing and Shanghai. These two regions were in the top 25 locations globally but neither came close to any of the top US clusters. Indeed, the US accounts for seven out of the top ten regions for biotechnology patenting globally (OECD PD). This is not surprising given China's low national presence in this area, as measured by both PCT patents and scientific publications. Possibly there is a great deal of high technology work being undertaken in China resulting in intellectual property that is protected through mechanisms other than international patents, but this seems unlikely.

The alternative explanation is that much of China's commercial R&D may actually be focused outside of high-technology areas. This may seem a counterintuitive conclusion, not least since much of the public debate about China in the West has focused on China's manufacturing capabilities and mounting production of high-technology goods. Yet there is interesting evidence to corroborate the notion that China is building innovative capacity in lower-technology domains.

In an earlier chapter, we mentioned the British Government's annual analysis of the top 1000 corporations globally by scale of R&D spending (DIUS 2010). Although the Chinese presence remains modest on this list, the number of Chinese firms has expanded over recent years. Twenty-one Chinese companies appeared in this ranking in 2009. They included well-known corporations like PetroChina, Huawei Technologies and Lenovo. When we categorise these firms by industrial sector, two striking attributes are evident: (a) their sectoral diversity and (b) the preponderance of activity in what are sometimes referred to as "low" or "medium" technology industries. Both these trends contradict the notion that Chinese competitiveness in innovation is especially focused on high technology and manufacturing.

The top 1000 list mentioned above illustrates the emergence of strong and active firms in several areas of information and communications technologies. On the 2009 list, the Chinese telecommunications equipment manufacturer Huawei Technologies reported greater R&D expenditure than did Apple. Generally though,

Chinese firms still rank lower globally than the leading firms in information and communications technologies. Among technology hardware and equipment manufacturers, Huawei Technologies, China's leading firm by scale of R&D investment in this sector, was still only ranked 14th globally.

Furthermore, there are gaps in other high-technology sectors. No Chinese aerospace, biotechnology or pharmaceutical firms appear on this list. There is only one firm involved in Internet technologies, software or computer services: this is Tencent, a firm with relatively modest R&D expenditures. The lack of Chinese firms investing at high levels on R&D in Internet technologies, software or computer services is particularly interesting since the greatest profit margins in the contemporary information and communications technology industries are typically to be found in precisely these areas, that is, in software development rather than hardware development (IBM 2010).

Perhaps most curious of all are the areas where China has the strongest firms by scale of R&D investment relative to the rest of the world: construction, oil and gas production, and mining. Firms that stand out in this regard are PetroChina, China Railway Construction, China Petroleum and Chemicals, China Communications Construction, and China Coal Energy. For many people this would be an unexpected development, as the sectors in which these firms operate are not usually highlighted in Western analyses of emerging Chinese innovation, especially in public or political discourse about the competitive threat posed by China. This strength implies that, while China's higher-technology capabilities are still developing, it is in lower-technology areas that Chinese firms have established their more competitive investments in innovation.

One should be wary when interpreting these trends. It is possible, for example, that those responsible for compiling these rankings are missing Chinese firms due to a scarcity of public data. It is also possible that there are many Chinese technology firms whose scale of R&D investment is just shy of that required to make the cut to appear on this list. By contrast, firms like PetroChina and China Coal Energy, with their strong links to the state, may lack the same level of competitive discipline in their R&D operations as may be true within some other sectors. These issues and uncertainties should qualify the conclusions one draws from these rankings. Nonetheless, the indications ought to temper impressions of Chinese technological power.

Let us also make some observations about the geographic distribution of the Chinese firms in this top 1000 list. Consistent with the patenting data, several of the leading firms in the technology hardware and equipment sector and in the electronic and electrical equipment sector are headquartered in Shenzen,

Guangdong. This is clearly emerging as a genuine cluster of high-technology innovation, not just for China—for the world. Beyond Shenzen though, around half the Chinese companies on the list have their headquarters in Beijing. It seems unlikely that these firms also perform the bulk of their R&D in that capital. Nonetheless it may say something significant about the political involvement of the Chinese innovation system that so many of these firms have their headquarters clustered around the political capital of the Chinese state. It's a stretch to imagine that the US would have become the global power it is today if a high proportion of its research-intensive firms had been headquartered in Washington D.C.

In the next chapter, we will elaborate upon the risks inherent in the various political dependencies that have emerged within the Chinese innovation system. But first we should underscore that China's innovation capacity is spread across a wide range of industries, and that China's successes are best understood in regional rather than national terms. The former point implies that there may well be more innovation occurring in China than outsiders recognise. The second point has an opposing implication: the ten eastern coastal provinces that dominate China's R&D investment account for a population not much greater than that of the US. For the moment at least, the real innovative competitor for developed nations is not China itself, but a subsection of it, and even within this subsection the potential is highly variable. Only in one Chinese province, Guangdong, can it be confidently stated that a globally significant high-technology innovation cluster has emerged.

4.4 Innovators in other nations will find uneven opportunities and ongoing uncertainties in China

The evidence presented should temper views of what has already been achieved in China. It may also qualify perceptions about the extent to which China already represents a competitive threat to the US. The explosion in the numbers of Chinese educated workers and researchers implies a mounting capacity for creativity and also for sophisticated consumption. But the intellectual property outputs from China do not yet suggest global leadership in technological innovation, and most regions in China are not yet seriously engaged in the development of globally significant innovations.

Some interesting implications for people and organisations in other nations follow. First, it's likely that many creative and talented Chinese will continue for some decades yet to sense that there are better opportunities to employ their talents outside of China. Seeking mechanisms for tapping into China's human capital will continue to be an important strategy for nations, corporations, and public-sector research organisations outside of China.

Second, there is little reason yet for outsiders to suspend their natural scepticism about Chinese intellectual property. Bit by bit, the quality of China's leading intellectual outputs will match those of the leading outputs produced elsewhere, but sorting the wheat from the chaff will not always be easy. Exercise of due diligence is especially important when evaluating any proposition involving intellectual property in China.

Finally, it would seem rational for outsiders to recognise that Chinese innovation is often regionally clustered. Foreign firms involved in China are already aware of this: they know where their suppliers, customers or competitors are located. But the same may not be true for policymakers or public administrators. For governments and public organisations seeking to develop international collaborations, there may be advantages in focusing on the scientific and technological institutions of a particular region rather than on those that exist across China as a whole.

The overall impression that the data engender about Chinese innovation is one of heterogeneity and uncertainty. Obviously things have changed rapidly over the past decades and may continue to do so. Chinese policymakers are certainly active proponents of a more innovative economy. The current model of economic development in China overtly expresses the need to foster "indigenous" Chinese innovation. But it seems premature to imagine that Chinese innovation is about to shape the world the way British innovation did during the eighteenth and nineteenth century, or the way American innovation did during the twentieth century. Those seeking a new intellectual frontier are most likely to find it the place they last saw it—the US. The idea of China as the world's dominant technological power remains a valid proposition, but a distant one.

5. The Questionable Value of Authoritarian Government

Has the Dragon emerged as a technological superpower? The answer apparently is no—or rather, not yet—especially when comparisons are drawn with the US. But will it become so in the foreseeable future? China is a technologically ambitious country and it is very easy to feel a sense of determinism about China when one considers the breathtaking reality of what has been achieved so far. After all, the evidence shows that China has raised its international visibility in the production of science and technology. China is now entrenched as a significant participant in the global production of knowledge. It has rapidly increased its share of global scientific publications and of international patents. Hundreds of thousands of Chinese students graduate every year as scientists and engineers, both domestic and foreign institutions. At the same time, surging productivity has driven a truly remarkable manufacturing export boom that has shaken the global economic system. Given that all these trends point in the same direction, isn't it just a matter of time before China achieves global technological pre-eminence?

In answering this question, two broad perspectives are offered. One possibility is that the rise of China is increasingly underpinned by a surge of genuine innovation and by an expanding stock of knowledge. Under this optimistic model, economic growth following the reforms of the past three decades has clearly enabled greater investments in knowledge, which in turn are now poised to trigger a fresh round of productivity enhancements and further economic growth. If one takes this perspective, China now faces "science and technology take-off" or, as the Chinese Government presents it in its tenth five-year plan, the country is about to become an "innovation economy" (Hu 2008).

However, there is another possibility: that the economic rise of China has enabled Chinese policymakers to construct a façade of dynamism and innovation that is not entirely genuine. According to this model, the growing economy in China has enabled Chinese policymakers to purchase all the trappings of a technologically sophisticated society: public institutions that churn out scientific articles, firms that invest in growing patent portfolios, and businesses that export high-technology manufactured products. But important questions remain about the quality of all these publications, the value of these patents, and the level of Chinese innovation embedded in their exports. Under this sceptical model, there is a much weaker sense of increasing returns from innovation or of mounting innovation intensity in Chinese society.

Like so much about China, the evidence is ambiguous. As we have seen, the scale of Chinese R&D investment and the growth in Chinese patenting activity does suggest a genuine growing technological capability. The global success of companies like Huawei Technologies and Lenovo testify to a re-emerging technological and entrepreneurial mindset in parts of China that is consistent with the concept of an "innovation economy". Yet the growth in business R&D expenditures and numbers of researchers in China may also reflect a growing willingness by business leaders to game China's tax system, which offers healthy tax credits for R&D activity. Likewise the dramatic boom in domestic utility patents, where the barriers to acquisition are fairly low, may also reflect social or political fashion rather than a demonstrable and transformative transition in Chinese innovative capacity.

In all likelihood, the realities for China combine aspects of both scenarios. Real innovation clearly does exist, but its distribution (both geographic and sectoral) is still somewhat patchy, and the same fast pace of change that has been experienced in China over recent years will not continue inevitably in the future. A sensible assessment of the facts should allow room for both optimistic and sceptical interpretations.

And yet there is evidence that a growing proportion of people around the world have already made up their minds. A recent survey of global attitudes performed by the Pew Research Center in the US reveals that around half those surveyed in Western Europe already see China, not the US, as the world's leading economy. Americans themselves are more likely to believe that China is the world's leading economy than to recognise that they are living in it (Kohut 2011). Even more telling is a KPMG survey, which finds that nearly a third of global technology business executives now identify China rather than the US as the most likely locus for disruptive innovative breakthroughs with global impacts. In this survey, nearly half of those asked projected that Silicon Valley would lose its reputation as the world's most dynamic technology innovation cluster within four years, with the most popular new location being cited as somewhere in China (KPMG 2012).

The wisdom of crowds may be revealing something here that is not yet apparent in the statistics; but it may also be reflecting a contemporary prejudice, which couples an instinctive anti-Americanism with an excessively sanguine interpretation of Chinese history. It has become common in the West to imagine that China's future will be bright not just because of its recent trajectory, but also because of a perception of China's historical role in the global economy, and a tendency to think uncritically about Chinese society and its system of political economy. For centuries China was the largest economy in the world and for a time it was one of the most technologically sophisticated. In these circumstances, it is understandable to view China's current rise simply as a restoration of the natural order of things. China is also perceived in the West as having benign—even enlightened—leaders. These factors reinforce bullish perspectives on China's innovation potential, but both warrant closer scrutiny.

5.1 Is it China's historical destiny to become the world's great innovating power?

Today the US economy is the world's largest national economy, but it has only been so for about 130 years (Maddison 2006). The size of the US economy first exceeded that of the UK and India in the 1870s and then surpassed that of China in the 1880s. Throughout much of the preceding millennium, China was the world's most populous country and also the world's largest economy—larger indeed than Europe and North America combined. China was technologically sophisticated. It is widely acknowledged that the Chinese have a proud history of discovery and invention (Needham 1954). Chinese technological supremacy prior to the European Renaissance is well documented. The Chinese famously invented gunpowder, the compass, the modern horse collar, and the iron plough—and they were using all these inventions a very long time before people elsewhere. Remarkably, the Chinese invention of paper took about a millennium to reach Europe and the Chinese invention of moveable type predated Gutenberg by about 400 years.

Even in the key technologies of the Renaissance and the Industrial Revolution there is evidence that China once had an early lead over Europe, which, curiously, it failed to exploit. It has been argued, for example, that Chinese water-powered spinning machinery in the fourteenth century was superior to anything in Europe prior to 1700 (Mokyr 1990). There were elements used in the construction of Chinese ships prior to 1400 that were not adopted by European shipbuilders until the nineteenth century (Mokyr 1990). And the Chinese output of iron in the eleventh century was equivalent to the entire iron production of Europe in 1700 and to almost twice that of England at the start of its Industrial Revolution (Jones 1981, McClellan 1999).

These historical details are persuasive. If China has been both rich and inventive in the past, it is only natural to ask why should it not be so again? It is possible even to believe in some sense that China "deserves" it, that what's happening here represents a return to some older natural order that was disrupted by the Industrial Revolution. In other words, the long view of global economics makes it (at least superficially) straightforward to imagine that an economically resurgent China will soon also overshadow the US in technological prowess. Moreover, such an interpretation seems especially plausible at this time of lingering economic crisis in the US, when pessimistic imaginations are given to pondering the impermanence of empires.

But historical patterns are seldom so straightforward. Comparisons of economic activity relative to population indicate that China has never really been exceptional in the way of the US or Europe. As we have discussed, what sets the US apart from other societies is not the scale of its economy, but its tremendous productivity. For most of the twentieth century, the US accounted for more than a fifth of global gross domestic product, but only because its share of the global economy was consistently more than four times its share of global population. No other society has ever brought such high relative wealth per capita to such a large population over such a long period of time. This capacity for extraordinary economic productivity has deep historical roots. From at least the early nineteenth century, the US has accounted for a high share of the global economy relative to its population. In Western Europe the trend goes back much further: it was producing an elevated level of economic activity relative to its population as early as 1500, well before the start of the Industrial Revolution (Maddison 2006).

This pattern contrasts sharply with that observed historically in China. Perhaps the most striking feature of China's modern economic history is the drastic collapse in China's share of world economic activity from the early nineteenth century. In the early nineteenth century, China accounted for around a third of the world's population and around a third of the world's gross domestic product. But by the mid-twentieth century, China accounted for more than a fifth of the world's population but less than a twentieth of the world's gross domestic product (Maddison 2006). Set in this context, the partial restitution of China's share of global economic activity (since the early 1970s) is a welcome development, and in some sense, we can view this as a partial restoration of China's historical place in the world economy after two centuries of political turmoil.

But if the Chinese aspire to have a truly innovative economy, then they will need to do something that they have never done before: they will need to account, as the US does, for a disproportionately large share of global economic activity. Here the historical evidence does not convey a sense of inevitability. If the most striking feature of China's recent economic history was the collapse in China's share of the global economy during the nineteenth and twentieth centuries, the more concerning, consistent and long-term observation is that China has never previously experienced sustained, elevated levels of gross domestic product per capita. For most of the past two millennia, China has accounted for 20-30% of world gross domestic product, but only because China's share of the world economy has tracked closely with its share of world population (Maddison 2006).

This implies that China's growth has been driven historically mainly by the sheer scale of its population. Yes, China may have had a previous history of economic strength and inventiveness, but it does not seem to have had a history of joining these two attributes together to profound effect, that is, converting its inventiveness into disproportionately large economic activity. This is not to say that China cannot evolve such a capability. Indeed, there is considerable evidence that China is now learning to do just that. But one should question the perception that there is an historical inevitability about China's transition into a powerhouse of innovation with the potential to rival the US.

Contrary to what is often said in the West, and contrary to what is now taught in Chinese schools, China's future economic and technological leadership is not a natural and inevitable chain of events. There are still many issues of uncertainty, including those relating to the nature of Chinese society and to its system of government. Indeed, a deeper analysis of Chinese history reveals evidence of several constraints that may eventually hold China back.

5.2 The lessons from China's history are not promising

When assessing the reasons for China's ongoing transformation it is worth remembering that many of China's key advantages are not new developments. China's population has always represented a potential market opportunity for innovative business people and entrepreneurs. China has always harboured an abundance of people with the educational levels and entrepreneurial capacity necessary to profit from this potential market opportunity (Rawski 2008b, Rawski 2011). Yet for much of its history, Chinese society has not seized this opportunity. Presently, China's strong technological growth trajectory and its rapid economic development provide much to marvel at, but the really extraordinary thing about China is the sustained period of economic stagnation and anaemic technological growth preceding this.

To be explicit, for most of its history China has been an important empire. For hundreds of years, China had a unified market, a commercially integrated economy and a well-educated workforce. Yet for hundreds of years, all of this has failed to generate rapid technological progress. China's problems in this respect predate Maoism, the Second World War, and its fraught relationships with colonial powers during the nineteenth and twentieth centuries. Between the fifteenth and nineteenth century, China managed to grow its economy but regressed technologically. As Joel Mokyr, an historian of economics and technology writes: "From the rise of the Ming dynasty in 1368 until the end of the nineteenth century, the Chinese economy expanded primarily through population growth, deforestation, commercial expansion, and ever growing intensification of agriculture, in an environment of increasingly stagnant technology." (Mokyr 1990)

On one level, there is nothing surprising in this. Technological inertia has been the norm for most societies in human history. By comparison, technological dynamism is the uncommon pattern of economic development. Yet there is evidence that China came close to industrializing in the fourteenth century (Jones 1981). It would seem that the potential for dramatic technological change in China has existed for a remarkably long time, and this returns us to our two opposing perspectives on the present.

For the optimists China's past technological stagnation is merely a phase, like the Dark Ages in Europe, which is surely now past. Korea and Taiwan have shown that relatively impoverished Asian societies can transform themselves into prosperous and technologically creative economies in a relatively short time. The conclusion for this camp is obvious: China's long overdue moment in the sun has arrived. For the sceptics, however, the deeper implication is not that China's turn has finally come but that Chinese society still has a considerable way to go before it can match the developed world's innovation and technological creativity. This group will question why China's transformation has taken so long, and they will conclude that while China may now be heading in the right direction, it may yet find itself beset by unforeseen obstacles. After all, if the vagaries of history have consistently constrained China from realising its potential in the past, then surely there is a possibility that this may happen again.

In choosing between these two perspectives, there are several reasons to side with the optimists. The circumstances for China are clearly more favourable than they have ever been. One of the explanations for China's historical failure to industrialise is that China was constrained by a lack of natural resources, specifically by the separation of Chinese population centres from coal deposits (Pomeranz 2000). This circumstance no longer impedes China's growth. By opening itself to global trade, and by expanding its own internal mining operations and internal trade, China has increased its use of coal exponentially since the 1970s. Indeed, China is now a much greater consumer of this particular resource than either the US or Europe (EIA 2010).

A related explanation is that China suffered simply by cutting itself off from the world. To some degree this was a function of geography. China is ringed along its inland frontiers by difficult terrain: mountains, deserts and steppes. Relative to Europe, China may have also suffered disproportionately from the debilitating, isolating effects of war and disease. China has had to contend periodically with the disruptive incursions of militaristic nomads along its northern frontiers, and the impacts of plague and war during the pivotal fourteenth century were arguably more devastating in China than they were in Europe (Pacey 1991). Thankfully, war and pestilence do not currently appear to threaten China's stability as they once did.

The isolation that various Chinese regimes have imposed upon themselves has also been a serious impediment. In the early fifteenth century, China led the world in maritime technology with bigger and better ships than were then available in Europe. Chinese naval expeditions explored the Indian Ocean and Africa's east coast sixty years before the Portuguese. But government-sponsored shipbuilding shuddered to a halt in 1419, and government opposition to maritime exploration meant that Chinese naval expeditions ceased completely after 1435 (Pacey 1991). In similar vein, during the seventeenth century when Jesuits first sought to introduce European science and technology to China, the Chinese downplayed the value of what they were receiving. Instead of serving as the precursors for a new worldview and a new economic system, clocks and telescopes in China became mere playthings in the imperial palace (Elman 2008).

As the historian David Landes posits, Chinese belief in their own cultural, moral and technical superiority meant that the Chinese failed to learn from other societies. He has argued that pride in their own achievements and the denigration of others cost China as much as four hundred years of technological progress (Landes 2003). Chinese isolationism was presumably compounded by a system of government that favoured individuals with literary rather than technical interests. The Chinese examination system and bureaucracy almost certainly channelled talent away from entrepreneurial and technological endeavours. Even more significantly, it created an intellectual elite that lacked both the interest and the understanding necessary to promote technological development (Mokyr 1990).

The contrast with contemporary Chinese society could not be more pronounced. Chinese international students now travel the world in vast numbers, actively seeking out educational opportunities and ideas, and the Chinese back home have become such avid users of foreign technologies that they are routinely accused of intellectual property theft. (See for example, Augustine 2007.) The Chinese political elite is no longer the preserve of the literati; it includes engineers and scientists to a degree unusual in the West. More broadly, China's new higher educational system seems to favour the production of engineers and scientists over graduates with humanities or social science degrees.

A profound signal of China's new openness is the prevailing Chinese attitude to globalisation. Over the past five years, the Pew Research Center has polled Chinese and American citizens annually about their attitudes to trade. When asked whether trade is a good or bad thing, around 90% of Chinese people surveyed reported that it is a good thing, compared with only 60-70% of Americans (Kohut 2011). No doubt opinions expressed in this survey were influenced by the turbulence experienced in the American economy since 2007. The results may also be heavily biased by regional factors in China. Nonetheless, it certainly appears that Chinese isolationism is a thing of the past.

What remains then for the sceptics? Are there any other lessons in Chinese history that might lead us to question the durability of China's new technological ascendancy? The overarching issue for Chinese innovation is the role of the Chinese government, or more specifically, the relationship between China's political system and its economic system. Even prior to the twentieth century, China has been consistently ruled through an authoritarian system of government and periodically this has led to two important constraints on innovation: inefficiencies in capital allocation, and the repression of creativity. Both these points are discussed below.

5.3 China's innovation potential will ultimately be constrained by its system of government

For good and bad, a key feature of China's economic history has been the role of government in production and, by implication, in the development of technology. During the early phase of the Song Dynasty, from 960 to 1126, a strong central government run by a meritocratic bureaucracy was able to interact effectively with independent entrepreneurs and Buddhist monasteries in order to stimulate a series of innovations in metallurgy, construction and textiles. Some of the technical achievements of this period were not matched in Europe for six hundred years (Pacey 1991).

Yet the experience of the Song Dynasty appears to have been the exception rather than the rule. An authoritarian system of political economy can move decisively and can be very effective when it gets things right; but it can also be hugely destructive when it gets things wrong. Today, one sometimes discovers an admiration in Western countries for China's capacity to move quickly in building major infrastructure. But when they are politically motivated, such projects do not always return benefits commensurate with their costs. During the early nineteenth century an English mathematician and statesman called Sir John Burrow estimated that there was as much stone in the Great Wall of China as there was in "all the dwelling houses of England and Scotland" (quoted in Waldron 1983). Although the Great Wall of China is often portrayed as a symbol of Chinese achievement, the cost to build it in terms of treasure spent and lives expended can also serve as a warning of how wasteful governments can be in their direction of human and capital expenditure.

Perhaps China's future prospects should be interpreted in this context. Over the past decade, the main source of growth in China's gross domestic product has not been exports but investment, and there is an emerging view that this investment is increasingly wasteful (Pettis 2011) and destabilising for the global economy (IMF 2011). According to this perspective, China's financial structures and policy settings have preferentially channelled investment to large infrastructure projects and to politically favoured firms, while suppressing household incomes and constraining employment growth (Prasad 2011).

This draws into question the Chinese government's attempt to foster innovation-based growth. To put it one way, China has created an economy that does not reward efficiency and that does not properly serve the welfare of the people within it. Put another way, by raising reservations about the long-term viability of China's current financial markets and institutional arrangements, these analyses suggest that modern China has still not established an economic system that will channel resources in those directions most likely to lead to innovation.

Of course, China can address this by moving further along the continuum from central planning to a fully-fledged market economy, but China suffers from a different, altogether subtler problem than that of overt central planning. Throughout much of its history, "collusion rather than dictatorial centralism was the mark of the Chinese system" (Jones 1981). Even in a context of ongoing market-based reforms, a risk for any society controlled by authoritarian government is that political collusion (and the subordination it breeds) is rarely conducive to innovation. Insofar as China's merchant class remains dependent upon the bureaucracy and insofar as the potential for commercial success can be determined by political decision-making, China's prospects as an innovative society will always face an inherent limitation.

This limitation will become more apparent as China's economy moves closer to the innovation frontier. Authoritarian regimes can successfully promote technological catch up, but their successes ultimately tend to be constrained because such regimes possess an intrinsic tendency to repress creativity. To innovate often requires an act of insubordination. Many companies are now allowed to operate in China as if they were free enterprises, but to what extent are their freedoms guaranteed? What happens when firms start to create products or to pursue goals that are inconsistent with the desires of China's political class? An authoritarian government may be more likely than a democratic one to restrict freedom of thought and freedom of action—and innovation, which can be thought of as applied creativity, requires both. However, this issue goes beyond the potential for active repression and beyond even the undercurrent of subordination that is created simply by the fear of repression. The current model of Chinese development provides preferential access to markets and preferential access to capital for state-owned firms over private businesses. Even within the private sector, advantages tend to accrue to firms that are run by those with the right connections. Even in the absence of extreme repression, such a system of political interference may ultimately provide an upper limit on China's innovative potential.

In the previous chapter we discussed the potential of China's human capital. We argued that China's vast population represents a huge potential resource and we showed how the value of this resource has been steadily increasing through education. In the long run, China's citizens will only reach their creative and innovative potential if they are able to operate in an economic and political environment that does not constrain the most talented among them. In his landmark analysis of the

Industrial Revolution in Britain, the economic historian David Landes defines the principle of "selection by achievement" as one of the key characteristics of the modern industrial system. He suggests that a critical dimension of effective industrialisation is that "men are chosen, not for who they are or whom they know, but for what they can do" (Landes 2003). While this rule is applied imperfectly in every society, some come closer to the ideal than others. The Chinese system of political economy, in which entrepreneurs must associate themselves with the state and in which the members of China's new wealthy class are likewise victims of political pressures, would seem unlikely to operate according to stringent and unimpeachable meritocratic procedures.

This suggests that China is already failing to maximise the value of its human capital in a way, furthermore, that may be creating an unusual middle class — a politically connected urban professional elite as opposed to a politically independent social class. This group, entrenched as it is with the state, may prove less open-minded in pursuing business opportunities and less accepting of future economic reforms (such as are necessary in all societies from time to time) than would be true of a politically independent middle class. This implication is troubling for China's future innovation prospects.

Throughout much of recorded history, and certainly until about 1400, China was an economic and technological powerhouse. It has never lost its potential in this regard and, in recent years, it has dramatically accelerated its innovative capacity. But the Chinese political system has never fully trusted the Chinese consumer or the Chinese entrepreneur. China's recent model of government has concentrated power, both politically and economically, and while it has leveraged this power to promote innovation very quickly along certain dimensions, an important constraint remains. By giving precedence to stability over freedom, to political rather than meritocratic processes, and to a subservient professional class rather than a politically independent middle class, the Chinese state has strengthened its own power at the expense of the country's long-term innovative potential. If China aspires to become the world's most innovative economy, some trade offs will need to be made—and the value of liberty should not be underestimated.

5.4 Innovation intensity in China has been a consequence of economic growth, not enlightened government

One reaction to these arguments about autocracy and public-private collusion is that they don't really matter so long as China is "led by a reasonably enlightened group of people, as China is today" (Friedman 2009). But enlightenment today is no guarantee of enlightenment in the future. Consumers and markets possess a different interpretation of enlightenment than that espoused by intellectuals and public commentators, and even the most enlightened government official must operate with imperfect information. Perhaps most importantly, it is easy enough for leaders to appear enlightened when circumstances are favourable. It is not obvious that China's authoritarian system of government will continue to look quite so beneficent and supportive of innovation during an era of heightened political tensions or reduced economic growth.

On this score, the data on innovation intensity and, more explicitly, on China's R&D intensity are fascinating. Over the past two decades, the most technologically innovative nations have had business R&D expenditures of 2-3% of gross domestic product, while virtually all developed economies have had public (i.e. university and government) R&D expenditures in excess of 0.6% of gross domestic product. By comparison, China's R&D investment intensity in both the public and private sectors remains low.

In the business sector, China's R&D investment intensity has certainly been increasing. As a share of gross domestic product China's industrial R&D intensity has grown from well under 0.5% throughout the 1990s to more than 1.3% of gross domestic product in 2010 (OECD MSTI). This represents a significant transformation. China's intensity of investment in business R&D now exceeds that of the European Union. Yet China's intensity of business R&D investment is still around half that of Japan or South Korea, and it remains considerably lower than the intensity of business R&D investment in the US.

As China makes the transition to an "innovation economy" one would expect its performance by this metric to continue to converge with the US and Japan. The idea of increasing R&D intensity is certainly a part of the Chinese Government's Twelfth Five-Year Guideline. However, the nature of this transition should be given some context.

First, it should be acknowledged that China's recent growth in business R&D expenditure relative to the size of its economy was not unique. Among developed nations Australia underwent a very similar growth in business R&D intensity during the 2000s (OECD MSTI). While China's growth in total business R&D activity has been remarkable, most of the expansion in business R&D investment can be attributed to the growth in China's economy, not to rising innovation intensity.

Second, one cannot assume that the last decade's growth in Chinese business R&D investment intensity will continue indefinitely. During the best part of the 1990s, China's business investment on R&D as a share of its economy was actually fairly flat (OECD MSTI) and it is quite credible that at some point the intensity of business R&D investment will flatten again. Whether this flattening happens at a European level or at an American or Japanese level will have a significant bearing upon the ultimate importance of Chinese technological innovation in the global economy.

Chinese investment in public sector research and development (i.e. universities and government agencies) conveys another important reality. Part of the emerging mythology about China's innovation system relates to perceptions about its expanding public knowledge infrastructure and about the enlightened role of government in underwriting this investment. Recently the West has paid considerable attention to the myriad universities being built in China, to the multitude of ex-patriot researchers being attracted back home, and to the huge investments being made in building new public research laboratories. For example, Chinese strategic investment in instrumentation and facilities was held up as one of the risks to US competitiveness in a report entitled *Rising Above the Gathering Storm* and published by the National Academy of Sciences in the US in 2007 (Augustine 2007). Occasionally articles have appeared in the American media along the lines that China is experiencing an "outpouring of investment by the Chinese Government" (Wang 2010b), and that it is in the midst of a "high-tech spending binge" that is "lavishing billions of dollars on new facilities" (Einhorn 2002).

But to equate the scale of public investment in China with enlightened policy is to misread the situation. The scale of public investment in China is indeed impressive. As we have seen, China's public research infrastructure has been transformed over recent years, resulting in the expansion of China's university system and in the volume of China's scientific outputs. The best laboratories at Peking University, Tsinghua University, Nanjing University or Shanghai Jiao Tong University are now conducting research of a standard that can be favourably compared with the best university research anywhere. However, a gentle caveat must be understood with respect to all of this activity: a less favourable picture emerges if one studies the intensity of R&D investment in universities and government agencies as a share of the Chinese economy. From the early 1990s to 2008, as a share of the national economy, China's investment in public sector R&D actually remained fairly flat at around 0.4% of gross domestic product. In 2010 investment did reach 0.47% of gross domestic product, but this was still around two-thirds the rate of investment across developed economies or 0.72% of gross domestic product (OECD MSTI). In other words, one should not attribute the growth in investment in China's public research infrastructure over most of the recent period to some special vision on the part of China's political leadership or even to a structural shift that is reprioritising certain public goods in Chinese society. It was merely the underlying growth in the Chinese economy that engendered the expansion in China's university and public research sector.

This is not to criticise the Chinese approach. A country on China's scale can fund a number of truly outstanding institutions without sustaining a high intensity of investment. This is one of the advantages of economic scale and in a country that is still dealing with mass poverty, huge infrastructure issues, emerging inequalities and regional imbalances, policymakers clearly have bigger concerns than how much of the public purse to hand over to university or government research. There may even be advantages to economic development in not investing too strongly at this stage in public institutions since such an investment might attract individuals with technical abilities away from commercial enterprises. The key point is that the low intensity of investment ought to temper estimations of the scale and quality of China's public research system. It also ought to temper expectations about the likelihood of ongoing investment growth under more adverse economic or political circumstances.

Certainly China has already succeeded in creating globally competitive institutions in favoured cities like Beijing and Shanghai. It also inherited a large number of outstanding institutions in Hong Kong that continue to thrive. But it is not yet investing nationally in its public research infrastructure at an intensity that is distinctive by developed world standards; and it is by no means guaranteed that increasing the intensity of public investment in innovation will remain a political priority over the long term. For an emerging economy like China's, the link between economic expansion and increasing innovation intensity is neither necessary nor inevitable.

In time all of this may present a limitation, especially if China aspires to innovate not only through the process of imitating and improving upon foreign technology, but also by creating its own new breakthrough technologies. In recent times, some of the most exciting industrial trends to emerge in the US (for example, biotechnology and the Internet) had their genesis in fundamental public research. This magnifies the significance of China's relatively low intensity of investment in public institutions. It also raises an important question about China's even lower level of investment in basic research. In 2009 the US spent 0.55% of gross domestic product on basic research, compared with 0.08% of gross domestic product in China (OECD MSTI). Furthermore, Chinese investment intensity in this particular form of research has been flat for two decades and does not seem to be converging with that of the US or Japan.

China is still in a phase of development where innovation is usually synonymous with imitation, adaptation, and incremental improvement; but truly great innovating societies have always had a capacity to go beyond this. As the US did over and again during the last century, the most innovative nations do more than simply improve existing industries—they create entirely new ones. China has not yet reached the world's innovation frontier and one should be cautious about assuming, whether from history or from a belief in enlightened government, that it is destined to arrive there soon. For all the evidence of China's expanding R&D capabilities, China's capacity to innovate in profound ways likely remains limited. This is not to deny that such a capacity might be developed rapidly. Nor is it to dispute the economic value of more applied research or development. But it does suggest that Chinese innovators still have a considerable way to go before they will equal the creative capabilities currently found in the US. The data on innovation intensity also imply that Chinese policymakers are yet to face the really hard choices that will set them apart as truly enlightened leaders. China's technological and intellectual supremacy should not be seen as inevitable.

5.5 This is not the time to place unhedged bets on the Dragon

The potential for China to continue on its current positive trajectory seems strong. Throughout most of the past two millennia, China has accounted for a greater share of the world's economy than it does even today, and probably also for a greater share of the world's innovation. There is still plenty of capacity for China's economy to grow, if only to return to its historical levels of activity, and it seems credible to expect that China's innovative and technological capabilities will continue to improve in line with its ongoing economic expansion.

China's predominant advantage lies with its large population. Large populations create big markets, and big markets tend to magnify the rewards that accrue to technological innovators. Big markets have the potential to foster competition, which can promote innovation. The potential scale of China's market has also provided policymakers with a useful bargaining chip in negotiations with foreign corporations. Access to Chinese markets is often only granted to firms willing to engage in technology transfer to China. Having a large population doesn't just create a market opportunity for China—it represents a resource. All other things being equal, large populations have the potential to throw up large numbers of entrepreneurs and inventors. The scale of China's workforce also increases the capacity for specialisation and for associated efficiencies in manufacturing new products. The rapid development of densely populated cities, improved educational opportunities, and ready transport and communications infrastructure means that products can be traded easily and ideas readily diffused across China's entrepreneurial communities.

This is all very positive. Due to its vast scale, it seems obvious that China could eventually develop both greater demand for new technological products and greater inventive capacity than is true in developed nations, including even the US. But what *could* happen is not often synonymous with what *will* happen. The advantages of China's vast population provide a logical justification for growth and advancement, but they do not ensure its inevitability, and the lessons of history and the nature of China's current political system should colour assessments of China's ongoing transformation.

The history of Chinese invention has not been one of relentless, self-perpetuating gain of the kind that evolved in Europe midway through the last millennium. China's history has rather been one of early precocity followed by periods of stagnation and even retreat. It is very easy to construe the current Chinese economic story as the beginning of a new and ineluctably advancing wave of Chinese innovation, but the continuation of China's economic expansion and its increasing innovative intensity should not be seen as inevitable. Likewise, one should be cautious about attributing infallibility to those who run the Chinese state. There is still plenty of distance to travel before China becomes a true "innovation economy" and a multitude of poor decisions could be taken at a political level along the way. At some point, pivotal players within the Chinese political system may even discover that their interests lie in resisting rather than in fostering innovation.

The implication for other powers here is subtle. Chinese firms and organisations are clearly becoming critical participants in global innovation and technological development, but unhedged bets on the long-term dominance of Chinese innovation are not yet justified. In many circumstances, where organisations are compelled to make a choice, it would seem foolhardy at this stage to jeopardise American relationships in particular because of a belief in the unstoppable rise of Chinese innovation. It is easy to be seduced by all those Apple computers and cell phones designed in California but made in China, by the world's largest high-speed rail network, and by the dazzling brilliance of Shanghai's skyline. China will in all likelihood continue to develop in a positive way, but at some point the pace of change is likely to slow, and outsiders should be cautious in their expectations of China over the near term.

6. Confrontation

With the US still the dominant power in science and innovation, but with China an increasingly competitive challenger, the potential for confrontation between the Eagle and the Dragon has been steadily growing. This is especially obvious in the narrative surrounding military technology. Every time China demonstrates a new military technology, whether it is a stealth fighter, an aircraft carrier or a cyber warfare capability, the Western media tend to focus on the potential for confrontation. Confrontation is also an emerging theme in the commercial sphere, particularly given China's repressed currency and its burgeoning trade surplus with the US. The growth of the Chinese manufacturing industry is often portrayed (in a mercantilist vein) as a direct cause of industrial decline and job losses in the US. Capability in science and technology is always an implicit feature of such discussions. In the modern age, strategic and economic security is widely accepted to be dependent in part upon innovation and science.

Of course, science, technology and innovation are age-old themes for contest between nations. This holds today for the US and China, as it did for the US and Japan in the 1970s-1980s, and for the UK and Germany in the late nineteenth and early twentieth centuries. Any shift in the scientific or technological competitiveness of nations is likely to create potential for confrontation. The rise of new technological powers has often been inspired by nationalism, and often this rise elicits fearful, nationalistic responses from incumbents.

As the Chinese economy has grown and as China has increased its total national investments in science and technology, the potential for confrontation with the US over scientific or technological matters has broadened. Here we highlight four main areas of confrontation between these two nations relating to (i) the projection of power, (ii) market protectionism, (iii) scientific competition, and (iv) education systems. We begin with some observations about the role of technology in confrontations between the US and China in relation to the military capability of both nations.

6.1 Chinese espionage and cyber warfare capabilities present significant threats to American supremacy in military technology

Technology has always played a pivotal role in the projection of political power. In this respect, weapons technologies are fundamental and were surely among the earliest technologies invented by humans. Communications technologies enable politicians or political organizations to spread and to control their message. Both of these technological domains have been a recent source of confrontation between the US and China. Consider the very public confrontations between the US and China in the area of weapons technology. Between 2007 and 2011, the US Justice Department has prosecuted dozens of serious attempts to smuggle US military technologies into China (DOJ 2011). These have included (some successful) attempts to ship the following restricted technologies to China:

- radiation-hardened microchips for use in satellites and missiles
- combat-grade night vision devices
- technical data relating to precision navigation devices
- stealth missile exhaust designs
- components for military phased radar and missile guidance systems
- NATO communications encryption equipment
- optical targeting systems used in unmanned aerial vehicles, Abrams tanks and Bradley fighting vehicles
- thermal imaging cameras
- flight simulation technology

- space shuttle and rocket technologies
- amplifiers used in missile targeting systems
- autopiloting technology for use in unmanned aerial vehicles
- technical data on nuclear submarines and future US warship technology

Some of these cases made global headlines, to which end the example of Chi Mak is particularly instructive. Born in China but a naturalized American citizen, he had lived in the US for more than twenty years before he was prosecuted for espionage. He had a family and home in Los Angeles where he worked as an engineer with a subsidiary of the defence contractor, L-3 Communications. In March 2008 he was sentenced to more than 24 years in prison for transferring US naval warship technologies to China.

This story illustrates an important issue. Over recent decades, the US has welcomed, and indeed become dependent upon, Chinese immigrants in its technical workforce. This is a source of constructive collaboration between the two nations; but the role of the Chinese diaspora in the US has also magnified the potential both for outright espionage and for less serious forms of technology leakage. It is worth remembering that during the Cold War, and starting with the development of atomic weapons, a significant amount of Soviet technology was acquired illicitly from the

US. (See, for example, Baggott 2009.) A similar, illicit transfer between the US and China is underway today and will likely continue to be a source of discord for the foreseeable future. Military power is an important determinant of a nation's international influence and the rising technological sophistication of China's military is bound to raise concerns in the US. Moreover, where Chinese sophistication owes a debt to American ingenuity, the likelihood of tension is augmented.

A related cause of confrontation has been the Chinese development (and deployment) of new technologies for disrupting electronic communications systems. For many years the Chinese People's Liberation Army has been openly building information warfare or cyber warfare capabilities. These include software-based approaches for infiltrating enemy computer networks as well as physical weapons for disrupting satellite activity in space (Krekel 2009). Of course, China has every right to arm itself. That it should choose to develop these particular capabilities is not especially remarkable given the digital nature of modern warfare. What is remarkable though, and a source of considerable tension with the US, is the application of such capabilities during peacetime.

Official Chinese policy does not support web terrorism. In 2001 and 2002, after a spate of politically motivated attacks on global websites and computer networks originated in China, official Chinese government media sources stated that such activities would not be tolerated. More recently, China's anti-hacking laws have been strengthened and several Chinese hackers have been arrested. Yet there are links between the Chinese hacking community and the Chinese Government. There have been allegations that the People's Liberation Army has sponsored hacking competitions throughout China, and that the People's Liberation Army has exploited the civilian population to create Network Warfare Militia Units composed of information technology professionals and academics with strict security vetting arrangements (Krekel 2009).

At the same time, the scale, complexity and systematic nature of many of the cyber attacks directed out of China in recent years imply state-sponsored activity, as do the organizations and network systems being targeted. It is significant that where Chinese cyber attacks have been linked to data theft, the stolen data have mostly related to military information or government policies. Chinese hackers seem to have a particular interest in information that brings strategic and military benefit rather than commercial benefit. In one well-publicized example, Google announced in early 2011 that the gmail accounts of senior US officials and Chinese activists had been specifically targeted from a site in Jinan, home to an information reconnaissance arm of the People's Liberation Army. The Chinese Government denied any involvement in the incident, but the targets of this attack seemed rather more political than one would expect from coincidence.

These trends are a significant source of tension. There is a view among some leaders in the US Government that Chinese espionage now presents a direct threat to American technological supremacy in both an industrial and military context (Bartholomew 2007). This is compounded by an acknowledgement from members of the US Congress that advancement of Chinese cyber capabilities could be used to cause catastrophic damage to critical infrastructure around the world (Bartholomew 2007). Ongoing confrontation in the this area has prompted the Pentagon to conclude in its first formal cyber strategy that under some circumstances computer sabotage coming from another country should be seen as an act of war (WSJ 2011).

6.2 Government policies are exacerbating tensions relating to industrial and technological competitiveness

If the first source of confrontation relates to the role of technology in the projection of political power, a second flashpoint relates to the nature of government interventions in technology markets. There is extensive literature on the role assumed by the Chinese Government in steering industrial development in China. In this context, a particular ongoing source of bilateral confrontation relates to the perception that Chinese industrial policies, especially those that create non-tariff barriers to trade, are damaging American interests.

These issues are regularly summarized in the annual reports of the US-China Economic and Security Review Commission (Slane 2010). As they relate to technology and innovation, the substantive concerns are straightforward. First, there is the issue of discriminatory government policies. It has been argued that government procurement policies, so-called indigenous innovation policies, and policies that make market access conditional upon intellectual property transfer to Chinese firms are squeezing American technology companies out of some of China's domestic markets. Second, there is the issue of trade-distorting government interventions in financial markets. China's longstanding policy to suppress the value of its currency has punished US exporters, encouraged US firms to relocate production to China, and restricted the consumption choices of Chinese consumers. The short-term consequence has been a trade imbalance; the long-term consequence is the relocation of production expertise to China.

These are matters of confrontation that extend beyond questions of technological leadership or innovative capacity. Nonetheless they clearly have an important bearing upon the trade between the US and China around new technologies and innovative products. The truth of this is particularly obvious in the context of the

Chinese Government's stated policy goal of transforming China into an "innovation society" by 2020 and in the specific strategies it has selected to achieve this goal. China is currently implementing a complex web of industrial policies that are inherently confrontational, especially in relation to technology-intensive products and the treatment of intellectual property rights. These issues are of growing concern to US industry groups, whose spokesmen have become increasingly vocal in criticizing China's technological protectionism.

The US Chamber of Commerce has argued that China's existing industrial policies are "considered by many international technology companies to be a blueprint for technology theft on a scale the world has never seen before" (McGregor 2010). The Chamber has identified many aspects to this story but, given the recent dramatic escalation in domestic patenting activity in China, of particular note is the use of domestic "junk" patents as a mechanism for Chinese firms to contest international intellectual property rights. The US Information Technology Organization (a consortium of industry associations involved in information technology, semiconductors, software and telecommunications) has made similar claims. In a 2010 submission to the US Government the US Information Technology Organization wrote with astonishing forcefulness that "the appropriation of intellectual property in China has occurred on such a massive scale that it continues to influence international prices, disrupt supply chains, change business models, and probably permanently alter the balance between tangible and intangible values contained within commercial products" (USITO 2010). Their submission pointed to pervasive government interference in technology licensing, to government use of standards and regulations as effective trade barriers, and to inconsistencies in the prosecution of intellectual property piracy and counterfeiting in China.

Chinese responses to claims of unfair treatment, intellectual property theft, market manipulation and hidden protectionism take several forms, but here are the main arguments in précis. There is the argument that, despite what critics say, China is actually making progress. After all, didn't Chinese authorities shut down a counterfeit Apple store in 2011, and hasn't China signed up to World Trade Organization commitments? There is the argument that China just needs more time: in other words, that China is still a developing country and its policymakers are doing their best in a challenging environment. There is also the argument that Western organizations have long benefited disproportionately from their intellectual property and have a skewed sense of fairness. After all, Western firms look increasingly dependent upon Chinese markets for their profits, and they have always held back on transferring truly valuable intellectual property to Chinese partners. Finally, there is the argument that Western governments don't play fair either. For example, aren't American export control laws relating to military technologies counter-productive in light of the US trade deficit with China?

Obviously there are two sides to every disagreement. However, this one seems particularly serious because it has deep implications for the way the Chinese and the Americans view each other. Evidently some Americans now believe that the Chinese Government has systematically employed an arsenal of regulatory mechanisms to coax foreign firms into trading their technologies for market access in China, only to exclude them later from these very same markets in order to ensure that Chinese firms profit from their technologies. On this score, the countervailing belief in China is that pursuing such policies is simply in the best interests of the Chinese people. In other words, China's discriminatory industry policies are a source of self-righteous indignation on one side and a consequence of resentful nationalism on the other. In this context, it seems likely tensions relating to industrial and technological competitiveness will grow in the years ahead.

6.3 Scientific competition has the potential to compound tensions between China and the US

This brings us to the third area of potential confrontation: the escalation of scientific competition between these two powers. We have already discussed the emergence of China as a leading producer of scientific research in certain fields. This has not been a cause of confrontation in the past, but clearly science has emerged as an area of competition between the two nations and there is certainly potential for future confrontation in this area.

In symbolic terms, China's involvement in developing technologies for space exploration can be seen in this light. When the US ended the space shuttle program in July 2011, some Western media organizations drew comparisons with the growing investment by China in its space program. But this is just one example of a broader trend. Under China's "Medium to Long-term Plan for the Development of Science and Technology" announced in 2006, Chinese Government research policies are currently shifting resources into large-scale projects. The publicly stated intention of this shift is to enhance the quality and scale of research focused on problems of national significance for China. Yet a growing role for China in bigger-scale science projects can also be expected to exacerbate Western fears about declining American competitiveness. However there are complicating factors to consider when assessing the impact of these developments.

As discussed in previous chapters, China and the US have made quite different predictions about which fields of research will matter most in the twenty-first century. To some degree, the relative importance of the life sciences compared with the physical sciences will have a significant bearing upon the likelihood of scientific confrontation between China and the US. But in the short term the questionable quality of Chinese science is more important. This becomes all the more pressing where research is driven in accordance with a system of government that adopts a planning mentality, and where funding mechanisms are essentially political in nature.

With respect to this point, considerable caution should be used in comparing American and Chinese scientific outputs simply by volume. Over the past decade, China's share of global outputs has grown, as has the number of Chinese journals with international profiles. There were 138 Chinese journals listed in the Thomson Reuters Science Citation Index in 2010, up from 47 in 2000 (WOK 2011). Yet the vast majority of these journals still have low impact factors: they are equivalent to just a fraction of the thousands of American journals listed in this index, and more broadly, Chinese research is still not frequently cited in the wider literature.

Earlier our discussion compared Chinese and American research across a range of fields by each nation's share of the top 1% of publications by number of citations. This revealed an ongoing disparity in the performance of each nation's elite researchers. In areas of emerging competition it is interesting to observe that this disparity prevails even in the bulk citation statistics. If one counts how often not just the very best papers, but how often all papers from a nation are referenced in the scientific literature one can derive a measure of a nation's average as opposed to its elite performance. Such an analysis implies a far more vibrant research system in the US than in China, even in fields with the greatest bilateral competition.

Let us consider the evidence. Across all fields over this decade, Chinese research attracted a third the number of citations per paper as did American research, and half the number as Japanese research. This disparity is broadly reflected in the statistics for the fields of molecular biology, physics and chemistry. In molecular biology, papers published by Chinese scientists are cited less than a third as often as those published by Americans, while in physics and chemistry Chinese papers are cited only just over a third as often as American papers (ESI 2011). The latter two fields are significant since these are areas where China's volume of output is approaching that of the US. The field of molecular biology is doubly significant since this is an area where US research still occurs on a scale that dwarfs such research in China. In both cases, despite growing competition, these citation data imply that China does not yet possess a research system that threatens American dominance.

Of course much can shift in a decade. Given the changes that have occurred in China over recent years, and given that citation data will tend to favour papers published early on in the analysed period, the real disparities may not be so marked. The difference by this measure between China and other nations is certainly not as sharp as that between China and the US. Chinese papers published over the decade to 2010 have been cited just over half as often as Japanese papers in the global scientific literature. In physics, Chinese papers have been cited at nearly two-thirds the rate of Japanese papers (ESI 2011). The gap with other developed nations seems to be closing, even if the US still clearly outstrips China's performance.

It is also worth noting that China's citations per paper are not so low relative to the US in two fields of special relevance to Australia: geosciences, and plant and animal sciences. Over the past decades, papers in these fields with Chinese authors garnered half the number of citations as papers with American authors (ESI 2011). It should not be surprising that this was higher than the relative rate of citations accruing to Chinese papers in physics and chemistry. As illustrated by the Chinese firms listed in the top 1000 firms globally by R&D expenditure, Chinese organisations are just as likely to challenge American and Australian organisations in areas like geosciences, mining, and agriculture as they are in physics and manufacturing.

Nevertheless, our underlying conclusions appear sound. In most fields systematic differences remain between the US and China. This implies that flashpoints for competition will more likely arise over outputs from specific institutions or cities rather than as a consequence of the success of the Chinese research system taken as a whole. For many years to come, comparisons of research quality may actually foster a relaxed view of Chinese scientific competition from America, and quality of research will continue to present a challenge for Chinese policymakers.

Having recognised this, there is a disturbing undercurrent with regards to the quality of Chinese research. Accompanying the very rapid growth in Chinese scientific publications, reports of fraud within China's scientific community have escalated. In one recent instance, the editors of *Acta Cystallographica Section E* (published by the International Union of Crystallography) discovered more than 70 fraudulent crystal structures published in their journal by two Chinese researchers based at Jinggangshan University in Jian (Harrison 2010). The two scientists involved and their co-authors from around China subsequently agreed to retract 70 papers. This incident prompted a number of strident editorials, including one in *The Lancet*, whose editors wrote, "For Hu Jintao's goal of China becoming a research superpower by 2020 to be credible, China must assume stronger leadership in scientific integrity" (Lancet 2010).

In another recent high-profile story Chen Jin, a researcher at Shanghai Jiao Tong University, garnered prizes and significant funding for his semiconductor research until it was discovered that his much-touted "Chinese" invention was just a Motorola chip with the branding scratched out (Hao 2006). China does not have a monopoly on scientific fraud. Nonetheless, there is evidence that this sort of behaviour is more pervasive in China than previously imagined. When the China Association for Science and Technology surveyed 32,000 academic staff in China in 2009 it found that 56% were aware of academic misconduct by their colleagues and that 39% were uninformed about the "norms of scientific ethics" (CAST 2009).

The situation has not yet reached a point where it has become a cause for international confrontation, but such a situation might well evolve. It has been reported that Chinese physics papers have low acceptance rates in western journals such as *Applied Physics Letters* (Day 2010). This may reflect the low quality of a proportion of Chinese scientific outputs, as illustrated by the citation data after publication. But it may also be an indication of something more insidious. Evidence of fraud or plagiarism, which undermines trust in Chinese science, will cause western researchers to be more cautious about publishing Chinese scientific articles and to be hesitant about collaborating with Chinese partners. All this has the potential to foster competitive rather than collaborative instincts in the interactions between Chinese and American researchers, instincts that may only be mitigated through the maintenance of fairly deep personal relationships between individuals.

6.4 There is mounting perception of a contest in education systems

This brings us to our fourth area of potential US-Chinese intellectual confrontation: the quality of China's education system and the perceived value accorded to education in Chinese society. Here, widely available comparative data has provided American policymakers and educators with some fairly confronting evidence.

Through the Program for International Student Assessment (PISA), for many years the OECD has sought to make international comparisons of school students' capabilities in mathematics and science. These tests are now used to measure the knowledge and skills of 15-year-olds across more than 70 nations or regions, and China has recently begun to participate by allowing student testing in three cities: Shanghai, Hong Kong and Macao.

It should be said at the outset that there is a good justification for selective regional testing in China. Educational standards vary considerably across the country, and one has to be cautious in making international comparisons based upon these data. Many developed nations also have an internal diversity in their educational performance. In the US, there is known to be considerable variation in performance by state, although this information is not published in the PISA database. Contrasting the performance of students living in a cosmopolitan city like Shanghai with the average performance of students in a nation of over 300 million people seems destined to exaggerate perceptions of national difference. Also, even if a small proportion of the US population excel at these tests, this proportion may still represent a large number of people due to the scale of the American population. One should be careful not to draw sweeping conclusions from these national testing projects.

Nonetheless, there is a movement in the US that perceives evidence of inferiority in the American school system, especially with respect to science and mathematics, and identifies this as a looming problem for American competitiveness (Augustine 2010). It's easy to see why. Pupils from all three selected Chinese cities appeared to have a significant edge in educational attainment over pupils in the US in 2009. Even in Macao, the weakest of the three Chinese cities, the average proficiency of 15-year-old students is now higher than US students and equivalent to British students in science and to Australian students in mathematics (OECD PISA).

In Shanghai, students achieved spectacularly high scores. Shanghai's pupils recorded higher average scores in both science and mathematics than was true for any developed country including Finland, Japan and South Korea. The mean score in science for a 15-year-old pupil in Shanghai was 575, compared with 502 in the US, while the mean score in mathematics for a 15-year-old pupil in Shanghai was 600, compared with just 487 for a pupil in the US. Among all developed nations, only in Singapore did the top 5% of pupils match the proficiency in mathematics and science of the top 5% of pupils in Shanghai (OECD PISA). For those in the US who tend to couch international competitiveness as a clash of education systems, the evidence of outstanding educational performance in science and mathematics in Shanghai and Hong Kong, and of fairly weak educational performance in the US can only be confronting.

Despite this, one should not necessarily ready oneself for an educational arms race. It seems credible to assume that there are far more cities in China with an educational performance closer to that of Macao than to that of Shanghai. In rural areas, where the vast majority of China's population still lives, the disparities would be even greater. There are also differences between disciplines. In science education, the ranking of the US among participating countries changes dramatically if one looks at the top 5% of students rather than the mean score for all students. Unfortunately, American educational standards do look extremely weak in mathematics, not just relative to Shanghai but also relative to other developed countries, and this is a core capability for any technological society.

Mathematics education rather than science education may prove a favoured theme for discussion by nationalistic Chinese and declinist Americans in the years ahead. Perceptions about the education systems in the two nations may also build into an issue of contention in the broader debate about immigration. As we will see in our subsequent chapter on collaboration, there has been a massive migration of educated Chinese to the US over recent decades. To date, this trend has proved beneficial to both nations. Yet if either nation should come to question the direction and the extent of skilled migration patterns between China and the US, educational performance and investment will surely be raised as a sensitive issue.

6.5 US-Chinese confrontation relating to science and technology has largely negative implications for other nations

The existence of tensions or possibility of outright confrontation between China and the US is not a positive theme for any nation in the Pacific. Some of these developments are surely an unavoidable consequence of

China's growing economy. Some of the issues we have raised are loosely analogous to those debated in the US at the time of Japan's economic transformation. One can recall the tensions then surrounding government interventions in technology markets and the questions about the effectiveness of the American education system. However, the fact that those tensions subsided in time ought not to diminish the significance of contemporary Chinese-American confrontation.

Evidence of Chinese theft of American military technology provides a clear imperative for Western Pacific innovators to choose their customers and suppliers carefully. Certainly while innovation and research relating to national security remains an issue of severe tension between the US and China, those working in third-party countries and seeking customers or partners in the US should be very cautious about their connections with the Chinese in this area.

The industrial policies of the Chinese may be just as challenging and confronting for other Western Pacific manufacturing nations, like Japan, as they are for the US. Efforts to influence Chinese policies relating to intellectual property rights, access to markets, currency manipulation, or adherence to World Trade Organization commitments may be more constructive if made through a collective approach. National governments across the Pacific region may ultimately see benefits in following the lead set by Australia and

South Korea in signing free trade agreements with the US (and each other).

Ongoing scientific and educational competition between the US and China presents much less serious issues for third parties. Judging from our analysis, scientists in some other countries may need to be circumspect about the quality and integrity of their research collaborators in China. However, individual researchers are usually acutely conscious of these issues and highly effective at managing them for themselves. The graver consequence is that an ongoing contest between the US and China may intensify the pressure on other nations in the region to increase their own investments in education or in public research. This may prove beneficial for the societies concerned, but not necessarily. An educational "arms race" may lead to a rise in scientific and education standards across the region, but it could also produce rapid inflation in scientific and educational costs with only marginal beneficial impact on outcomes.

7. Collaboration

The US and China are sometimes portrayed as colossal powers with divergent interests whose future destinies are intertwined only insofar as they seem fixed on a collision course. Yet there is another interpretation of their interaction, at least as it relates to science and innovation: American and Chinese technological systems are increasingly mutually interdependent. Our proposition is that, despite an intensely competitive undercurrent, commercial and intellectual communities in the US and in China are becoming intermeshed in a thickening web of economic, scientific and personal connections. Consequently, the two societies are increasingly interlinked and evolving in highly interconnected ways.

In this context, two themes warrant discussion. The first is essentially an economic proposition: the opening of the Chinese economy and the export-led development strategy adopted by Chinese policymakers has created a powerful interdependency between these two nations. The second theme is largely demographic: mass migration of skilled workers has led to deepening links between American and Chinese research systems.

7.1 The US and China possess a strong commercial, technological and scientific interdependency

With respect to the first theme, it is useful to return to trade statistics. Trade is an important form of collaboration and over the past decade there has been an explosion in trade between the US and China, particularly relating to advanced technology products. The key trends may be summarised as follows: firstly, total volume of US trade (i.e. exports plus imports) with China in advanced technology products increased nearly sixfold between 2000 and 2010; secondly, much of this increase was due to a nearly tenfold rise in the volume of US imports of information and communications products and optoelectronics products from China; but thirdly, US exports to China of other advanced technological products (aerospace, advanced materials, biotechnology, electronics, flexible manufacturing, life sciences and nuclear technologies—all areas where the US actually has a trade surplus with China) also grew more than threefold over the decade (Census 2011).

As previously discussed, these statistics have become a source of some bilateral tension, especially in light of the enormous trade deficit that now exists between the US and China, and specifically in the trade of information and communications products. For those in the US who are concerned about a declining American manufacturing capability, the scale of the trade imbalance in this sector (exceeding $100 billion in 2010) is deeply troubling. Again, one should be cautious in interpreting these figures. A high proportion of China's exports still consist of its assembly capability for multinational companies, for which much of the value originates outside of China (Hammer 2011). Also the implications of these imbalances are surprisingly complex. Arguably, the policies that have helped to underpin China's trade surplus with the US have actually increased US-Chinese interdependency, even as they have strained US-Chinese relationships.

Exchange rate and monetary policies have assisted China in attracting foreign direct investment, in building manufacturing capabilities, and in expanding exports. There is an understandable perception that these advantages have been established at the expense of China's competitors. But these same policies have also supressed the purchasing power and purchasing choices of Chinese workers. They have restricted the role of Chinese consumers in underpinning domestic growth and, ironically, they have created an environment in which the interests of many Chinese firms and even the Chinese Government itself (which now holds a massive amount of American currency and bonds) are curiously connected with the stability and growth prospects of the US economy. These same policy arrangements have also provided massively advantageous price deflation for American consumers. Both societies now possess strongly shared incentives to see sustained, stable growth in the other (Prasad 2009).

The debate about trade balance should not overshadow another reality of the US-China relationship: whatever its net direction, the vast expansion of trade between these two nations in and of itself implies increasing economic interdependence. By 2010 China accounted for 33% of all US imports of advanced technology products and for 50% of all US imports of information and communications products. On the other side of the ledger, China accounted for 11% of all US exports of advanced technology products, and for a slightly lower share of US exports of information and communications products (Census 2011). These figures indicate a growing interconnectedness at the high-tech end of these two economies. They point to enhanced competition, yes, but also to a certain commonality of interest and to growing interaction. There is also evidence that the bilateral trade of goods and services has been accompanied by growing opportunities for the exchange of ideas. For example, economic interaction has led to a proliferation of formal bilateral agreements relating to research and innovation. US corporations have sought to integrate Chinese technical talent into their global innovation activities. One recent estimate suggests that over 300 companies in the Fortune 500 list have now set up R&D centres in China (Cao 2009). IBM, Microsoft, and Intel have been particularly active in this respect, as evidenced by the international patenting activities of their Chinese employees.

The activities of these firms can extend well beyond the sponsorship of isolated R&D facilities, as demonstrated by the actions of IBM. In addition to its basic research laboratory in Beijing (a facility involving 200 engineers, many of them PhDs) IBM has also funded a large number of laboratories in Chinese universities. IBM is also investing more broadly in software development capability throughout China and boasts of partners in literally hundreds of Chinese cities. This level of engagement by a high profile US technology firm has significant implications for policymakers in other parts of the Asia-Pacific who may have hoped to attract similar domestic investments from foreign corporations.

The priority that US firms have given to cultivating innovation capabilities in China and the matching Chinese appetite for attracting precisely this sort of investment is reshaping the nature of the trade in ideas between these two countries. The mode of technical interaction in the private sphere appears to be largely one of US investment in Chinese domestic innovation activity. By comparison, evidence of joint innovation activity involving engineers based in both China and the US is much harder to come by, as is evidence of direct Chinese investment in US domestic innovation.

Patent statistics illustrate this scarcity. In 2010, only around 9% of Chinese PCT patent filings involved a co-inventor who was resident in another country. This compared with over 25% for Germany and Australia, with nearly 50% for the US, and with 80% for Switzerland (WIPO 2011). It would seem that Chinese-based organisations are not especially open to technical collaboration with inventors based in other parts of the world.

There may well be cultural factors at play here. Levels of foreign collaboration appear low not just for China, but for Japan and South Korea too. Most East Asian societies have remarkably low rates of foreign co-invention in their international patents. However China is strikingly different from developed East Asian nations like Japan and South Korea in one important respect: a high proportion of PCT applications involving Chinese inventors are foreign-owned. Nearly 40% of PCT applications in 2010 involving a Chinese co-inventor were actually applied for from another country. This compared with fewer than 30% of PCT applications involving an Australian or Swiss co-inventor, around 20% of PCT applications involving a Germany co-inventor, around 9% for those involving a Korean co-inventor, around 8% of those involving a US co-inventor, and fewer than 4% for Japan (WIPO 2011).

These data underline two important elements of international technological collaboration involving China: technical collaboration between organisations based in China and inventors based elsewhere may be limited and certainly does not lead to many joint authorships on patents, and there is a high level of foreign ownership of globally relevant Chinese inventions.

The specifics in the case of the US-China relationship match this pattern, but are slightly more nuanced. Separate data collated by the OECD from the US Patent and Trademark Office, and the European Patent Office as well as through the PCT process suggest that applicants based in the US account for around a third of all non-Chinese patent applications involving Chinese inventors (OECD PD). In other words, organisations based in the US are important investors in Chinese intellectual property, although they are not the only organisations working with Chinese partners in this way. Where the US figures more decisively is in measures of co-invention. Examining technical collaboration rather than ownership, one finds that although foreign inventors are only rarely named in PCT applications involving Chinese co-inventors, when they are the majority turn out to be American. Over the past decade, well over 50% of Chinese inventions involving foreign co-inventors have involved a co-inventor with a US address (OECD PD).

Since our claims about collaboration are based simply upon the addresses of applicants and inventors in patent applications, they may be imprecise. These statistics won't detect instances where American inventors move to China temporarily and use a Chinese address in a patent filing. They will also fail to recognise foreign ownership where a foreign-owned firm applies for a patent using a subsidiary based in China—presumably a rapidly growing practice. However, in broad terms the data do seem to indicate that private-sector collaboration between American and Chinese partners is focused strongly within China itself. This is perhaps not the fluid, multi-nodal, open form of collaboration that one expects in a globalised world.

Realities are different in the public sector. There has been a proliferation in memoranda of understanding between Chinese and American government agencies. One recent estimate suggests around fifty such agreements were signed over the past decade across a very wide range of scientific disciplines (Wessner 2011). While many of these initiatives are largely symbolic, some have had significant funding attached. In July 2011, for example, a US-China Clean Energy Research and Development Center was announced through which the US and Chinese governments would each invest $75 million over five years for joint research into carbon capture and sequestration as well as energy-efficient vehicles and buildings. But these sorts of formal processes are not the main conduits for joint research. The grassroots actions of individual researchers in both the US and China have been much more important in driving scientific collaboration, and here the pattern is one of much greater openness and of a clear and strong flow of ideas between both countries.

The evidence in this respect is clearly illustrated in the extent to which scientists from both societies now co-author scientific articles. From 1995 to 2010, one striking trend in the global scientific literature has been the growth in the number of joint publications by American and Chinese researchers. In 1995, researchers based in China were co-authors on only 3% of internationally co-authored articles published by researchers based in the US. This made China the thirteenth most important partner to the US research system. Indeed, Chinese scientists that year were co-publishing fewer papers with US researchers than Australian scientists were. Yet by 2010, Chinese scientists were co-authors on 14% of such articles, a greater proportion than any other nation (NSF 2012). In other words, China is now the most important source of international co-authors for American research.

Chinese science is becoming increasingly useful then to researchers in the US, but this relationship is far more important for China itself. Over 45% of China's internationally co-authored scientific articles in 2010 had at least one American co-author—a staggering statistic. This proportion was significantly higher than that of developed nations and also significantly higher than that of China back in 1995. Even as China has expanded its own public research system, it has deepened its interconnections and interdependence with the US.

The extent of China's scientific collaboration with the US is very unusual. After the US, China's second most important collaborator is Japan. Yet whereas American researchers were co-authors on just over 45% of Chinese internationally co-authored articles in 2010, researchers from Japan co-authored just 10% of China's internationally co-authored scientific outputs. China has not yet integrated its research system with other nations on anything like the scale of its integration with the US system. Whereas American co-authorships account for over 25% of the internationally collaborative scientific outputs of most developed nations, Chinese co-authorships still account for fewer than 10% of the internationally collaborative outputs of other nations (NSF 2012).

Two exceptions to this rule are worth noting. Singapore is the only nation with a greater level of collaboration with China than the US, as measured by co-authorships. This is perhaps unsurprising for cultural and ethnic reasons. Australian scientists also collaborate more with China than most European nations. Australian scientists were co-authors on 5% of internationally co-authored American papers in 2010, and co-authors on7.5% of internationally co-authored Chinese papers (NSF 2012). Australia is the only western nation whose co-authorships account for a higher share of China's scientific output than for its share of the US's output, lending a special relevance to its relationship with both these powers. Of the three other nations playing a larger role in China's collaborative output than that of the US, all are Asian: Japan, Taiwan and Singapore. This may imply that Australia's particular relationship with China reflects its location on the periphery of Asia. It may reflect a time zone effect. Of equal significance is the probable role of ethnic Chinese researchers in the Australian public research system, and there are strong analogies to be drawn here between Singapore and Australia and the US.

7.2 The importance of the Chinese diaspora

Any consideration of the relationship between China and the US, and of their growing interdependency must account for the role of Chinese migrants. The Chinese diaspora has been vital for research collaboration between China and the US. Mass migration of scholars has occurred from China to the US. For decades, large numbers of Chinese students have studied in the US and the vast majority of them have chosen to make the

US their home. This trend extends back to the 1980s. Following the Tiananmen Square protests of 1989, the US Government granted 70,000 Chinese migrants permanent residency in the US and a significant number of them have pursued scientific or technological careers (Biao 2008).

Furthermore, over the twenty years since 1989, almost 60,000 Chinese students have graduated with PhDs from American universities and the total volume of Chinese students pursuing research degrees in the US remains extraordinarily high. An analysis of the number of foreign PhD students graduating from American universities in 2009 shows that nearly 4,000 Chinese nationals earned doctorates at US universities, nearly double the number of Indian nationals, three times the number of South Koreans, eight times the number of Canadians, and almost twenty times the number of Germans (NSF 2012). China is easily the most significant source of international scholars in the US, although by this measure India is expected to supplant China in the years ahead.

The proportion of Chinese PhD graduates intending to stay in the US following their studies is also striking. Over recent decades, the number of Chinese students receiving PhDs from American universities has grown steadily, topping 4,500 in 2007. This total now seems likely to decline due to demographic effects as well as the creation of new and improved educational opportunities in China. But equally important is the question of whether those who do graduate in the US choose to remain in the US or return to China. Over 90% of Chinese graduating doctoral students intended to remain in the US in 2003. Since that time, this proportion has declined slightly. Yet even in 2009, the proportion intending to stay in the US remained extraordinarily high, at over 80% (NSF 2010). This figure is remarkable, especially when one considers that in 2009 opportunities for PhD graduates had never been better back in China, and the US economy was in turmoil following the 2008 financial crisis.

To a great extent this migration pattern has driven science and innovation collaboration. Migration has been fundamental to the American economy since the founding of the first British colonies, and migration associated with the technical education of scholars from Asia has been a well-documented aspect of this story. Chinese immigrants have been an important part of this larger phenomenon, making powerful contributions to American innovation. One recent study has suggested that migrant entrepreneurs ran a quarter of the technology firms founded in the US between 1995 and 2005 (Wadhwa 2007). The role of Chinese entrepreneurs was not so significant as that of Indian entrepreneurs over this period, but Chinese entrepreneurs were especially active in California, and in the computing and communications sectors.

Furthermore, Chinese migrants have been the most visible migrant group involved in US inventions. In 2000, 13% of the scientists and engineers in Silicon Valley were of Chinese origin. From the late 1990s to 2006, Chinese nationals based in the US were listed as inventors on US patents filed through the PCT process more often than migrants from any other nation (Wadhwa 2007).

Although the significance of the Chinese migrant workforce in the US is widely understood, less well appreciated is the growing role of this community in building links and in transferring capital and skills back to China. It is important to note that Chinese scientists co-publish much less often with their colleagues in Europe than they do with their colleagues in the US. Indeed, this is true even when one normalises for the size of the scientific community in the US and in Europe. The much larger Chinese diaspora existing in the US probably explains this disparity. One recent analysis suggests that over 70% of US-China co-publications in maths, physics, chemistry and biology have at least one American-based co-author with a Chinese name (Jin 2007). Many co-ethnic publications in the molecular life sciences have also be reported, again based on surnames, confirming that the size of Chinese scientific communities in partner nations is an important determinant for the scale of co-publication with researchers based back in China (Jonkers 2009).

In the academic sphere, the role of the diaspora is no doubt accentuated by recent growth in the population of Chinese migrants deciding to return to China. As discussed, this is indicated in the modest increase in the proportion of Chinese PhD graduates choosing to leave the US following the award of their PhDs. But more important perhaps is the cohort of high-performing individuals who, having succeeded in the US, choose to accept co-appointments in China or to travel there frequently and share expertise. In both public and private sectors, evidence is emerging of a new transnational professional class of individuals who travel regularly between the US and China, maintaining links and sometimes joint residences in both nations (Saxenian 2006). These cross-regional entrepreneurs are a dynamic and powerful force that can be expected to foster growing collaboration and interconnections between the Chinese and American innovation systems for years to come.

This community's values, vibrancy and political influence seem likely to have long-lasting consequences for the evolution of innovation systems in the US and China. In relation to science and technology, the behaviour of this community will prove pivotal in ensuring that the US and China find more reasons to collaborate than confront. Connecting with this community may also prove increasingly valuable for outside innovators seeking to build their own links to China or to the US.

7.3 US-Chinese collaboration in science and technology is largely positive, although there is a risk it will become exclusive

The growing integration of the American and Chinese economies can be seen as a promising development for the Pacific region. It shows that different languages, cultural practices, religions and systems of government can be gradually bridged. The thickening web of connections between these two powers implies a regional future that can be peaceful and harmonious—an obvious benefit for all concerned. But the integration of the Chinese and American economies is positive in another sense. As expanding trade (and exchange of ideas) forces both countries to identify their areas of comparative advantage, the development of innovative products across both major economies may continue to accelerate, bringing ongoing, indirect benefits to consumers everywhere.

But there is a risk that the expansion in American-Chinese interaction will occur at the expense of interactions with other nations. It is arguable that the recent wave of investment by US firms choosing to establish R&D centres in China has come at the expense of investments that might otherwise have occurred elsewhere in the region —in nations such as Australia, Singapore, or even Japan. The strengthening ties between Chinese and American businesses have raised the stakes for business leaders and policymakers in smaller nations seeking to attract high profile US technology firms into their own domestic economies.

A similar narrative may be unfolding in the growth of joint American-Chinese patenting activity and co-authorship of scientific publications. This development is beneficial to China and to the US, and also broadly beneficial in that it accelerates the general advance of scientific and technological discovery. But the growing numbers of Americans and Chinese working together may diminish the collaborative opportunities available to inventors and scientists in other nations. Nothing has been of greater importance in facilitating commercial and scientific collaboration between the US and China than the Chinese diaspora. This network of relationships has been pivotal in expanding the range of scientific and technological options available to both nations. Yet the very richness and binding strength of this network could also serve to exclude outsiders. This is a sobering prospect for other countries in the region, especially for those lacking a community of well-educated and entrepreneurial ethnic Chinese. To offset this, other nations' drive to engage or strengthen connections with the Chinese diaspora may prove vital.

The critical implication for Western Pacific nations is that their citizens should not take their relationships with China or the US for granted. Scientists, inventors and policymakers throughout the Pacific should be aware that a strengthening of ties between China and the

US carries risks as well as benefits. In certain situations, those who work in scientific or technological roles may need to redouble their efforts to connect to partners in either China or the US. Scientific and technological communities in smaller Western Pacific nations may need to work even harder to ensure that they are linked to the leading research networks in the US.

8. Between the Eagle and the Dragon

To the south and east of China, along the western rim of the Pacific Ocean, a group of nations is wrestling with what it means to exist between the Eagle and the Dragon. Ranked by gross domestic product in 2010, these nations include Japan, Australia, South Korea, Indonesia, Taiwan, Thailand, Malaysia, the Philippines, Singapore, New Zealand, Vietnam, Cambodia and Papua New Guinea. Culturally, politically and economically, they are highly diverse societies and yet these 700 million people share one very important attribute: their future prosperity and security will be heavily influenced by the fortunes of both the US and China.

Of course the nations in this group interact with China and the US in different ways. Some of these countries like Australia and Indonesia are rich in mineral resources and currently enjoy exciting trade opportunities with China. These opportunities may seem to erode the relevance of commercial links with the US. Other countries like Japan, South Korea and Taiwan have already built strong commercial links with Chinese manufacturing firms. Indeed, these nations have played an integral role in building manufacturing capability in China, yet they balance this with a broad strategic and political alignment with the US.

Behind these differences are common problems. If they are wise, the people who live between the Eagle and the Dragon will hope that both powers will prosper; but if they are realistic, they will acknowledge that one of these societies may ultimately surpass the other. Investors, business leaders and policymakers will feel pressure (or the temptation) to place bets on the success of one of these two economic superpowers. Indeed, there will be times when an informed judgement must be made as to which economy, which society, or which nation to back.

The information we have presented suggests that, despite China's remarkable trajectory, the balance of power in technology and innovation still resides with the US. However, in assessing the potential for future leadership in innovation within these two economies, there are some striking uncertainties with important consequences for Western Pacific nations.

8.1 Which power will be more effective at stimulating innovation in an era of persistent uncertainty?

Allowing that the future economic and innovative capacity of nations is notoriously difficult to predict with accuracy, it may be confidently asserted that technologically creative societies generally meet three conditions: they nurture resourceful innovators who have the will and skills to challenge the status quo, they have institutions that provide incentives for innovation, especially relating to wealth and status, and they are open societies willing to overturn vested interests and tolerate changes to the status quo.

Let us consider whether the US and China are nurturing resourceful innovators who have the will and skills to challenge the status quo. It is apparent from our analysis that American and Chinese societies have developed fundamentally different priorities in their education and public research systems. China is graduating large numbers of PhDs and engineers, and public research has been heavily focused on the physical and quantitative sciences. By contrast, the American system has produced higher proportions of social scientists and liberal arts graduates, and has given a higher priority to public research in the medical and life sciences.

In terms of disciplines, it is too early to know which society has made the more astute bet. Judging by what happened in the twentieth century (when physical sciences and engineering proved fundamental to transforming innumerable industries) one would have to side with China. However, it may be that in the twenty-first century innovations in the life sciences and in the social sciences will generate greater returns. Regardless of these different trends in scientific discipline, the more important unknown is whether China is nurturing true innovators or merely developing an army of technical experts.

It is customary to associate technological dynamism with the discovery of new technologies, that is, with inventions. By cultivating specific forms of technical expertise and through its "indigenous innovation" policy, China's workforce strategy purports to value local invention, but can it promote dynamism? Over recent years China has been exporting inventors (mainly to the US) and importing entrepreneurs (most notably from Taiwan). This may reveal a flaw in the Chinese model. While the talents, skills and education of specific inventors can constrain invention, innovation is more constrained by the social network, that is, the behaviours of entrepreneurs, consumers, regulators, and so on. It is easy enough for a government to avow a policy and build an inventive skill-base by investing in expertise, but the nurture of innovative capabilities is never so straightforward. China's potential in this respect remains a significant unknown, especially when innovation thrives by questioning the status quo.

In Britain around the time of their Industrial Revolution, Daniel Defoe observed that the English were largely copiers of other people's ideas. They were entrepreneurs rather than inventors. Even a century later, after eighty years in which British manufacturing accounted for two thirds of Europe's growth in industrial output (Bairoch 1982), a consultant engineer called John Farey told a British Parliamentary committee on patent law that "the prevailing talent of English and Scotch people is to apply new ideas to use and to bring such applications to perfection, but they do not imagine as much as foreigners."

In other words, what made Britain distinctive were not its scientists and inventors so much as its entrepreneurs and innovators. The same has arguably been true of American society. It is worth noting that America's entrepreneurs are typically much more visible than its inventors. People like Bill Gates, Steve Jobs, Mark Zuckerberg, Jeff Bezos and Larry Page are widely admired household names in the US. In contrast to the situation in China, the US model has arguably been one of importing inventors and breeding entrepreneurs. This model may well be more advantageous for nurturing innovation.

Our second condition involved the provision of incentives for innovation. Innovation requires individuals to take risks, but individuals are typically risk-averse unless they stand to gain wealth or status by taking an alternative position. Competitive markets provide intrinsic incentives for innovators. The desire to motivate your customers to buy your products rather than your competitors', and do so while preserving a decent margin, clearly acts as an important incentive for innovation. In this respect, China's economic reforms of the 1980s have increased incentives considerably. Governments also provide regulatory incentives for innovators, most obviously through their intellectual property laws and tax systems. The recent strengthening of China's intellectual property system and the indebtedness of the US Government (which implies a US need to grow taxes and thus reduce incentives for their own innovators) will likely reduce the historical disparities that have existed between China and the US in these domains.

Deeper uncertainty arises from the incentives for innovation that may be embedded within the social structure. This is a compelling issue when considering the political implications of the expansion of China's middle class. Most of the early industrialists of the British Industrial Revolution were drawn from the middle class, a class for whom careers in government and the military were largely closed. They found an outlet for their creativity and a mechanism for acquiring wealth and ultimately status in trade and commerce. The US, too, is largely a middle class nation. Bourgeois values dominant in American culture include a belief in private property and the rule of law, a tendency to equate the accumulation of wealth with self-improvement rather than greed, and a belief in moral independence, in other words, a belief that all people ought to enjoy liberty as independent citizens rather than live in servility as government subjects.

The expansion of China's middle class implies the expansion of a community that values participation in trade and industry, and accords not just financial rewards but also social status to those who build their fortunes independent of the state. The growth of the middle class is a very positive development for Chinese innovation. However, the level of Chinese political support for middle-class values remains uncertain. Particularly concerning are perceptions of arbitrariness in the rule of law. If the financially successful come to feel that the fruits of their labours are vulnerable to political confiscation or to politically motivated changes in business conditions, then the incentives for innovation will weaken. More broadly, if the Chinese social system ultimately affords greater status to those who work within the Communist Party or within the machinery of government than it does to those who generate wealth through commercial activities outside of government, then again the incentives for innovation will be weakened.

This is not to suggest that there aren't similar uncertainties in the US. If the US political class pursues a trajectory to develop a European-style social security system, fostering entitlement values rather than middle-class values, then the US will become a nation of dependents rather than a nation of entrepreneurs, and its prospects for leading the world in innovation and technology development will dim. It is also possible that a new generation of Americans, energised by a liberal arts education, will simply lose interest in making products or providing services for others and will choose instead to channel their talents into political activities or other public sector roles where rates of technological innovation are low. However, this would seem a less serious risk in American society than in China, where it is easy to imagine the country's rapidly shifting social structure stimulating detrimental political reactions that discourage and ultimately punish entrepreneurs. The extent to which incentives for innovation are embedded within the Chinese social system is not yet known.

This brings us to the value of openness. Technologically dynamic societies tend to be open to changes to the status quo. They also tend to be open to ideas and to people from other places. Tolerance is a critical virtue here. One of the great strengths of Britain during the Industrial Revolution was its propensity for welcoming foreigners with technical abilities, regardless of their religion. Then, Britain attracted European migrants in much the same spirit, albeit in much lower volume, as the US attracts migrants from all parts of the world today. One of the under-appreciated strengths of modern China is that it too has recently evolved into a migrant society. First, there is the mass migration occurring internally, from the countryside to the cities and from the West to the East. Second, there is the migration of the Chinese global diaspora outwards to the educational institutions of Western nations, and then back again to China. Both of these trends can be expected to increase tolerance for new ideas within Chinese society.

Whether the political machinery in China can nurture and complement this openness remains unknown. Innovations and new technologies have winners and losers. The Chinese political system currently supports technological change in a generic sense because this is aligned with its interests—but this may change. There is a risk that the Chinese government's autocratic instinct and political obsession with stability will lead directly to policies that restrict innovation.

But there is an equivalent risk across the other side of the Pacific. Technological creativity is aided by the conviction that the exploitation of science and the application of practical knowledge will make the world a better place. Western societies have consistently been at their most innovative when their participants shared a belief in progress, when they perceived technological development as virtuous, and when they have desired to create and enjoy that which is new. Confidence in what is new is pivotal for any society's capacity to absorb innovations. In this respect, a telling comparison can be drawn between China and Europe during the Industrial Revolution. At this time, a Jesuit missionary to China, Louis Le Comte contrasted Chinese and European attitudes towards progress, noting that the Chinese "are more fond of the most defective piece of antiquity than of the most perfect of the modern, differing much in that from us, who are in love with nothing but what is new" (quoted in Landes 1998). In a historical role reversal, today a Chinese migrant visiting Europe may be inclined to make the reverse observation about contemporary Europeans, although as yet they'd be unlikely to think in this way about Americans.

This could change. In many Western nations today, including the US, political environmental movements are actively upending the idea that technology is virtuous and are questioning the belief that a future driven by technological innovation will always be better than the past. In this respect, contemporary environmental philosophy is arguably pushing Western culture in precisely that direction which once constrained technological innovation in China. In 1922, the distinguished Chinese scholar Feng Yu-Lan published an extraordinary essay entitled "Why China has no Science" (Feng 1922). He argued that Chinese intellectuals were constrained by their values: they were more interested in spiritual development than material development, they were more interested in creating harmony between people and their environments than in recreating their environments. Later in the twentieth century, Joseph Needham made a similar argument. He also identified "harmony" as a motif of Chinese philosophy, arguing that the Chinese worldview promoted coexistence with nature rather than subjugation of nature, implying this may in part account for the differential rates of technological progress in Europe and China during the modern era (Needham 2004).

It is possible that we are now approaching a new era when the East, including China, is steadily becoming bent on the pursuit of materialist goals through technological transformation—just as the West, including the US, is beginning to find technological progress distasteful. An acceleration of these trends would result in a permanent shift of technological power and innovative capacity from the Western to the Eastern nations. Such a scenario seems unlikely for the US at the moment, but it's not impossible. The future cultural distribution of different attitudes towards technology and the natural world is an area of significant uncertainty, which could have a profound bearing on American and Chinese leadership in innovation.

In summary, the political, cultural and social uncertainties that will help to determine the future innovative performance of the American and Chinese economies make predictions challenging. Destabilising events in the global economy, changes in the international political landscape, and even natural disasters could shape the future for both of these societies in unanticipated ways. In this context, it is impossible to state with confidence how either nation will develop technologically over the coming decades. This challenge is exacerbated by new scientific discoveries and by the ever-shifting nature of technological opportunity.

One of the more interesting hypotheses about Britain's Industrial Revolution is that it occurred because eighteenth-century Britain possessed a unique combination of high wages and low energy costs (Allen 2010). Indeed this combination of factors has been used to explain the persistence of technological advantage in the West across nearly four centuries since the start of the Industrial Revolution. There is evidence that we are at the start of a new cycle of industrial innovation driven largely from the US and empowered by a similar set of economic circumstances. Wages in the US remain very high by global standards. At the same time, energy costs appear to be falling. The potential to tap vast unconventional gas shales using new hydraulic fracturing technologies is extremely significant in this respect and may herald a new period of innovation in the US in which access to extremely cheap energy enables manufacturers to find new ways to replace labour with capital. This potential is further augmented by the rapidity of advances in computer processing and software development, swiftly escalating the scope and sophistication of automation technologies. Under these circumstances, it is possible to imagine an increase in US comparative advantage across many areas of manufacturing. It is also credible to imagine a reduction in Chinese comparative advantage for the same reasons. In China there will be weaker incentives over the coming years for replacing cheap labour with energy-intensive technologies. China may even experience an erosion of comparative advantage in areas where today it is considered a particularly strong competitor.

In short, we are living in an era of persistent uncertainty. Evaluating the prospects of both China and the US is an extremely complex and challenging undertaking. It is certainly premature to write off the US, which remains the preeminent technological power and the most innovative nation. Nor is it possible to deny the rapid and dramatic emergence of China as a competing scientific power and as a nation with growing technological capability, not only in information and communications product manufacturing, but also in lower-technology areas such as construction and mining. The challenge in evaluating the relative prospects of both powers is also exacerbated when one considers the extent to which these two societies are becoming dependent upon one another, commercially and scientifically, despite their intensely competitive undercurrents.

8.2 Some recommendations for Western Pacific nations

Given all this, it seems likely that innovators in other countries will discover that they need to connect effectively with both the US and China. This may pose a problem for Pacific nations. Whether they are interested in accessing markets, developing products or collaborating in the creation of new ideas, organisations across the Western Pacific clearly need strategies that will enable them to balance their relationships with both the Eagle and the Dragon. Obviously, what this means in practice will vary depending on an organisation's or an individual's specific circumstances. At the national level, much will depend on local advantage and culture. After all, the nations of the Western Pacific can also be considered as diverse creatures in their own right, and they bring different kinds of value to potential partners and customers in China and the US.

Consider the following three models:

(i)   Australia's open to all comers model. Australia shares its language and many of its cultural values with the US, and its researchers have a long history of engagement with the American research system. But Australia also has an active and growing community of ethnic Chinese researchers, an overlapping time zone, and complementary trade interests with China.

(ii) Japan's commercial model. Japan has a historically fraught relationship with China and a marginal Chinese diaspora. On one hand, it has developed a fairly strong strategic and political understanding with the US. On the other hand, it has formed a dynamic commercial association with both the US and China, underpinned largely by the unique, innovative manufacturing capabilities of its firms.

(iii) Taiwan's pragmatic model. Taiwan shares a language with China and is populated by Chinese migrants, many of them the descendants of those who fled from communism. Politically, Taiwan uses a strategic relationship with the US to balance China's claims to Taiwanese sovereignty. Yet the basis of its interactions are pragmatic: the electronics industry in Taiwan has established deep networks back to Silicon Valley and across the Taiwan Strait to Shenzen.

Differences in local situation will necessarily frame the relationships that are stimulated across the region.

Notwithstanding these differences, it is possible to point to some underlying principles. Innovators in the Western Pacific will generally find it easiest to connect with partners in the US and China in areas where they have a specific cultural connection or where they have something distinctive to offer. It is across these two dimensions that local factors will most likely exert themselves. But these are not the only factors. Partnerships between organisations in Western Pacific nations and the US and China will also reflect the changing domains of comparative advantage across the US and China.

The idea that any country, no matter how large, can dominate innovative activity across every sector of industrial activity seems unlikely. One credible conclusion from our analysis is that China and the US can each be expected to possess shifting areas of commercial comparative advantage over the coming century. We can already observe this in a couple of key sectors: today, those seeking to find world-leading capabilities in services still need to look to the US, while those seeking centres of innovation in certain areas of electronics manufacturing will be better served by looking to Asia, including China.

The size of China's domestic market and its workforce implies that a comparative advantage in innovation relating to the mass production of many consumer goods will continue steadily to shift to China.

But nothing is certain. This trend may be undermined if other low-cost producers in the developing world begin building their own competitive manufacturing capabilities, as already seems to be occurring in South-East Asia, or if rising Chinese labour costs shift the economics for manufacturing in the US, or if changes in other input costs such as energy lead to a renaissance in innovation among American producers.

As we have stressed, for competitors and trading partners across the region, there is an inherent unpredictability here. In all likelihood, areas of distinctive comparative advantage in innovation will continue to emerge for both China and the US, but such patterns may prove relatively fluid over time. This potential for changeability in the relative strength of US and Chinese innovation has serious consequences for Western Pacific nations. For one thing, it suggests that governments interested in developing internationally collaborative innovation programs with China or the US should be cautious about focusing on either party or on particular industry segments. If one accepts that American and Chinese innovation and competition will frequently shift across a range of industrial sectors, then it follows that societies across the Western Pacific will do best where they can respond nimbly and where their response is based upon relevant industry knowledge. This implies a much greater role for commercial organisations than it does for governments.

We should also reiterate that the heavily publicised rebalancing of Chinese and American manufacturing activity has obscured some interesting trends for those economies with a so-called low-technology orientation. For countries like Australia or Indonesia, which have historically developed a comparative advantage in sectors like mining, agriculture and construction, the growth in trade with China has been very visible. But the potential for collaboration and competition in these sectors should not be overlooked. Australian organisations particularly should expect steadily increasing competition from China in these domains, where there are already a number of very large Chinese firms operating. Public researchers should also anticipate growing interest in research collaboration across associated fields like the geosciences and the plant and animal sciences.

There are also conclusions to be drawn about the distribution of capability in basic research. Strengths within the American and Chinese public research systems are likely to depend on the future fiscal positions of central governments. The differences between national governments in this respect may well determine American and Chinese public research capability over the long term. As we have highlighted, there is already an important shift underway in the balance of power between China and the US across individual fields of research.

In fields like mathematics, physics and engineering, it is likely that researchers in Japan, Australia and South Korea will find more opportunities to collaborate with public sector researchers in China than with public sector researchers in the US. By contrast, although China's capability in the life sciences is growing, researchers across the Pacific seeking to work with the best researchers globally and hoping to maximise their links with the most influential knowledge networks in these fields would still be better served by focussing on their American partners. This is especially true for researchers seeking commercial opportunities in biotechnology. There may be future opportunities in this area in China, but for the time being both the market for biosciences products and the epicentres of invention and development expertise in the biosciences remain in the US.

It is also worth remembering that there will be indirect benefits from ongoing American and Chinese competition. For example, China's emergence as a manufacturing power and the ensuing intensification of global competition in technology manufacturing has led to sustained price deflation across a range of electronic components, information and communications products, and other high-technology devices. If this process continues, it will magnify opportunities for technology integrators and for engineers involved in the development of new products and services built around software rather than hardware. Under this scenario, Australian, Singaporean and Japanese innovators in the financial services and business services sector and in niche manufacturing sectors (such as the medical devices sector) may identify new and interesting opportunities. But in a more complex and competitive world, they may also need to work harder to define their competitive niche.

There will also be indirect consequences from the expanding depth of US-Chinese partnerships—and not all will be positive for outsiders. While the appetite for international collaboration in research has been steadily increasing for decades, the strengthening nexus between public researchers in China and the US could ultimately reduce incentives for these researchers to engage with colleagues in smaller Pacific nations. This nexus is reinforced by the role of the Chinese diaspora in the US, and may warrant active policy responses from governments in nations like Japan and South Korea. There, the strong tradition of connectivity with the US research system should be defended.

Such a development may indicate a need for policymakers to adjust the mechanisms by which they promote international collaboration. Most countries' traditional mode of engagement with the US in research and innovation has been relatively informal, based largely on personal interaction and perceptions of mutual opportunity. By contrast, with China there appears to have been a greater drive to build collaborations around formal agreements, often with government involvement. In an environment where interactions with both China and the US are important, policymakers may be wise to assess whether formal agreements with China are really leading to effective collaborations on a regional, sectoral, organisational or individual scale, and whether in certain areas there is a new space for formal agreements with American partners to increase the value of existing, grassroots collaborations.

More significant is the importance of migration. Effective international engagement in science and innovation usually has an intensely personal dimension, and it is hardly surprising that the Chinese diaspora in the US has been profoundly important in helping the US forge bridges with China, and vice versa. Chinese migration, largely driven by international education, has been of far greater strategic importance to US-Chinese relations than all the signed memoranda of understanding, or all the joint initiatives that the Chinese and American governments have ever embarked upon. Policymakers who understand this and are keen to increase scientific or technological engagement with either the US or China should make the flow of international students and scholars in all directions a high priority. But they should make their relationships with one another a priority too.

As we have noted, excluding China, there are 700 million people living in the nations of the Western Pacific.

It is worthwhile remembering that together these nations constitute a population twice that of the US and nearly equivalent to that of China. Policymakers, business leaders and innovators in these societies will miss opportunities if they become focused on fostering connections with the two regional superpowers at the expense of also building strong relationships with each other.

In conclusion, the emergence of China as an economic and technological power is a hugely positive development. It has brought unprecedented prosperity to millions of Chinese and it has brought unparalleled opportunities for trade to many nations. Furthermore, it is accelerating humanity's pursuit of knowledge and its capacity for creating new products and technologies. The benefits and opportunities implicit in these changes are enormous—and one hopes they will be sustained. But it would be a mistake for citizens of other Western Pacific countries to become distracted by the rise of China in such a way as to neglect the ongoing importance of the US or the opportunities existing elsewhere in the region.

Among policymakers and business leaders, the importance of China to the region's future is now widely accepted and frequently remarked upon. One hears far less often about the importance of building new networks, new product markets or new collaborations between Australia, Japan, South Korea, Vietnam and Indonesia, and one hears remarkably little about the need for innovators in some of these nations to continue to learn from the US. In time this may prove an oversight, a bias in our contemporary perspective of the world that we will some day regret. The sun has not yet set on American innovation, nor is Chinese long-term pre-eminence automatically assured. Naturally, the innovative and entrepreneurial members of other countries will take their opportunities where they may, but their greatest future opportunities may not reside where today's prevailing opinion expects to find them.

Bibliography

ABS 8104 — Australian Bureau of Statistics, *8104.0 Research and Experimental Development, Businesses, Australia, 2008-09*, 23 September 2010.

ABS 8112 — Australian Bureau of Statistics, *8112.0 Research and Experimental Development, All Sector Summary, Australia, 2008-09*, 11 October 2010.

Allen 2010 — Robert C. Allen, "Why was the Industrial Revolution British?", *Kuznets Lecture: Yale University*, 2010.

Anderson 2006 — Chris Anderson, *The Long Tail: How Endless Choice is Creating Unlimited Demand*, Hyperion, 2006.

Augustine 2007 — Norman Augustine et al., *Rising Above the Gathering Storm: Energizing and Employing America for a Brighter Economic Future*, National Academies Press, 2007.

Augustine 2010 — Norman Augustine et al., *The Gathering Storm, Revisited*, National Academies Press, 2010.

Baggott 2009 — Jim Baggott, *Atomic — The First War of Physics and the Secret History of the Atomic Bomb: 1939-49*, Icon Books, 2009.

Bairoch 1982 — P. Bairoch, "International industrialisation levels from 1750 to 1980", *Journal of European History*, 11:269-334.

Barlow 2008 — Thomas Barlow, *Innovation in America: A Comparative Study*, The United States Studies Centre at the University of Sydney, December 2008.

Bartholomew 2007 — Carolyn Bartholomew et al., "2007 Report to Congress", *US-China Economic and Security Review Commission*, US Government Printing Office, 2007.

Bhidé 2008 — Amar V. Bhidé, *The Venturesome Economy: How Innovation Sustains Prosperity in a More Connected World*, Princeton University Press, 2008.

Brandt 2008 — Loren Brandt, Thomas Rawski, and John Sutton, "China's Industrial Development", in Ed. Loren Brandt and Thomas G. Rawski, *China's Great Economic Transformation*, Cambridge University Press, 2008.

Brandt 2009 — Loren Brandt, Johannes Van Biesebroeck, and Yifan Zhang, "Creative Accounting or Creative Destruction? Firm-level Productivity Growth in Chinese Manufacturing", *NBER Working Paper 15152*, National Bureau of Economic Research, July 2009.

Branstetter 2008 — Lee Branstetter and Nicholar Lardy, *China's Embrace of Globalisation*, in Ed. Loren Brandt and Thomas Rawski, *China's Great*

Economic Transformation, Cambridge University Press, 2008.

Branstetter 2010 — Lee Branstetter and C. Fritz Foley, "Facts and Fallacies about US FDI in China", in Ed. Robert Feenstra and Shang-Jin Wei, *China's Growing Role in World Trade*, The University of Chicago Press, 2010.

Burrelli 2010 — Joan Burrelli, *Foreign Science and Engineering Students in the United States*, National Science Foundation, July 2010.

Cao 2009 — Cong Cao, Denis Fred Simon, and Richard P. Suttmeier, "China's Innovation Challenge", *Innovation: management, policy & practice*, 11:253-259, 2009.

CAST 2009 — China Association for Science and Technology, *Chinese S&T professionals believe misconduct in science a protruding problem in China today*, 17 July 2009.

Census 2011 — Census Bureau, *Foreign Trade Statistics: Country and Product Trade Data, Advanced Technology Products*, 2011.

CGS 2010 — Council of Graduate Schools, *Joint Degrees, Dual Degrees, and International Research Collaborations: A report on the CGS Graduate International Collaborations Project*, 2010.

Chesbrough 2003 — Henry Chesbrough, *Open Innovation: The new imperative for creating and profiting from technology*, Harvard Business School Press, 2003.

Day 2010 — Charles Day, "Physics in China", *Physics Today*, 33-38, March 2010.

Dedrick 2008 — Jason Dedrick, Kenneth L. Kraemer, and Greg Linden, *Who Profits from Innovation in Global Value Chains? A Study of the iPod and Notebook PCs*, Personal Computing Industry Center, July 2011.

DIUS 2010 — *The 2010 R&D Scoreboard*, Department of Innovation, Universities and Skills, UK, 2010.

DOJ 2011 — Department of Justice, *Summary of Major US Export Enforcement and Embargo Prosecutions: 2007 to the present*, June 2011.

EIA 2010 — US Energy Information Administration, *International Energy Outlook 2010*, US Department of Energy, July 2010.

Einhorn 2002 — Bruce Einhorn, *High Tech in China: Is it a threat to Silicon Valley?*, Bloomberg Businessweek, 28 October 2002.

Elman 2008 — Benjamin A. Elman, *A Cultural History of Modern Science in China*, Harvard University Press, 2008.

ESI 2011 — *Essential Science Indicators*, Thomson Reuters, 2011.

Eyman 1997 — Scott Eyman, *The Speed of Sound: Hollywood and the Talkie Revolution, 1926-1930*, Simon and Schuster, New York, 1997.

Feng 1922 — Feng Yu-Lan, "Why China Has No Science — An Interpretation of The History and Consequences of Chinese Philosophy", *The International Journal of Ethics*, 237-263, April 1922.

Florida 2005 — Richard Florida, *Cities and the Creative Class*, Routledge, 2005.

Fortune 2012a — *Most Admired Companies*, Fortune Magazine, 2012.

Fortune 2012b — *Global 500*, Fortune Magazine, 2012.

FT 2010 — *FT Global 500*, Financial Times, 2010.

Frank 1995 — Robert Frank and Philip Cook, *The Winner-Take-All Society*, The Free Press, 1995.

Friedman 2009 — Thomas L. Friedman, "Our One-Party Democracy", *The New York Times*, 8 September 2009.

Gibson 2008 — Rick Gibson and Nick Gibson, *Raise the Game*, NESTA, December 2008.

Hall 1999 — John Hall and Charles Lindholm, *Is America Breaking Apart?*, Princeton University Press, 1999.

Hammer 2011 — Alexander B. Hammer, Robert Koopman, and Andrew Martinez, "Overview of US-China Trade in Advanced Technology Products", *Journal of International Commerce & Economics*, 3(1): 1-16, May 2011.

Hao 2006 — Hao Xin, "Scientific Misconduct: Invention of China's Homegrown DSP Chip Dismissed as a Hoax", *Science*, 312: 987, 19 May 2006.

Harrison 2010 — William T.A. Harrison, Jim Simpson, and Matthias Weil, "Editorial", *Acta Crystallographica Section E*, 66(1):1-2, January 2010.

Hippel 1998 — E. von Hippel, *The Sources of Innovation*. Oxford: Oxford University Press, 1988.

Hippel 2005 — E. von Hippel, *Democratizing Innovation*. Cambridge: The MIT Press, 2005.

Hollister-Short 1976 — G.J. Hollister-Short, "Leads and Lags in Late Seventeenth Century English Technology", *History of Technology*, 10:31-66, 1976.

Hu 2008 — Albert G.Z. Hu and Gary H. Jefferson, "Science and Technology in China", in Ed. Loren Brandt and Thomas G. Rawski, *China's Great Economic Transformation*, Cambridge University Press, 2008.

Hu 2009 — Albert Guangzhou Hu and Gary H. Jefferson, "A Great Wall of Patents: What is behind China's recent patent explosion?", *Journal of Development Economics*, 90(1): 57-68, September 2009.

Hutton 2008 — Will Hutton, *The Writing on the Wall: China and the West in the 21st Century*, Abacus, 2008.

IBM 2010 — IBM, *Annual Report*, 2010.

IMF 2011 — International Monetary Fund, "People's Republic of China: Spillover report for the 2011 Article IV consultation and selected issues", *IMF Country Report No. 11/193*, 2011.

Interbrand 2011 — Interbrand, *Best Global Brands 2011: Creating and managing brand value*, accessed at www.interbrand.com.

ISI 2010 — *ISI Highly Cited*, Thomson Reuters, 2010, accessed at isihighlycited.com.

Jefferson 2008 — Gary H. Jefferson, "R&D and Innovation in China: Has China Begun Its S&T Take off?", *Harvard China Review*, 11 August, 2004.

Jenner 1994 — W.J.F. Jenner, *The Tyranny of History: The Roots of China's Crisis*, Penguin, 1994.

Jin 2007 — B.H. Jin, R. Rousseau, P.R. Suttmeier, and C. Cao, "The role of ethnic ties in international collaboration: the overseas Chinese phenomenon", in D. Torres-Salinas, H.F. Moed (eds), *Proceedings of the 11th International Conference of the International Society for Scientometrics and Informetrics*, 427-436, Madrid, 2007.

Jones 1981 — Eric Jones, *The European Miracle*, Cambridge University Press, 1981.

Jonkers 2009 — Koen Konkers, "Emerging ties: factors underlying China's co-publication patterns with Western European and North American research systems in three molecular life science subfields", *Scientometrics*, 80(3):775-795, 2009.

Kohut 2011 — Andrew Kohut et al., *China Seen Overtaking U.S. as Global Superpower*, Pew Research Center Global Attitudes Project, 13 July 2011.

KPMG 2012 — *KPMG Global Technology Innovation Survey*, June 2012.

Kraemer 2011 — Kenneth L. Kraemer, Greg Linden, and Jason Dedrick, *Who Captures Value in the Apple iPad and iPhone?*, Personal Computing Industry Center, July 2011.

Krekel 2009 — Bryan Krekel, George Bakos, and Christopher Barnett, *Capability of the People's Republic of China to Conduct Cyber Warfare and Computer Network Exploitation*, The US-China Economic and Security Review Commission, 9 October 2009.

Lancet 2010 — "Scientific fraud: action needed in China", *The Lancet*, 375(9709): 94, 9 January 2010.

Landes 1998 — David S. Landes, *The Wealth and Poverty of Nations*, ABACUS, 1998.

Landes 2003 — David S. Landes, *The Prometheus Unbound*, Cambridge University Press, 2003.

Lee 2007 — John Lee, *Will China Fail?*, The Centre for Independent Studies, 2007.

Maddison 2006 — Angus Maddison, *The World Economy*, volumes 1 & 2, OECD Development Centre Studies, 2006.

Matthews 2009 — Mark Matthews, Bev Biglia, Kumara Henadeera, Jean-Francois Desvignes-Hicks, Rado Faletic, and Olivia Wenholz, "A bibliometric analysis of Australia's international research collaboration in science and technology: analytical methods and initial findings", *FEAST Discussion Paper 1/09*.

McClellan 1999 — James E. McClellan and Harold Dorn, *Science and Technology in World History*, The Johns Hopkins University Press, 1999.

McGregor 2010 — James McGregor, *China's Drive for 'Indigenous Innovation': A Web of Industrial Policies*, 28 July 2010.

Mokyr 1990 — Joel Mokyr, *The Lever of Riches*, Oxford University Press, 1990.

Mowery 1999 — David C. Mowery and Nathan Rosenberg, *Paths of Innovation: Technological Change in 20th-century America*, Cambridge University Press, 1999.

Needham 1954 — Joseph Needham, *Science and Civilisation in China*, Cambridge University Press, 1954.

Needham 2004 — Joseph Needham, *Science and Civilisation in China, Volume 7: The Social*

Background, Part 2: General Conclusions and Reflections, Ed. Kenneth Girdwood Robinson, Cambridge University Press, 2004.

Nobel 2008 — *Nobel Foundation Directory*, accessed during October 2008 at http://nobelprize.org/.

NSF 2010 — National Science Board, *Science & Engineering Indicators*, 2010.

NSF 2012 — National Science Board, *Science & Engineering Indicators*, 2012.

NSF 2008b — National Science Foundation, Division of Science Resources Statistics, *Business R&D and Innovation Survey*, 2008.

OECD 2011 — OECD, *National Accounts of OECD Countries*, accessed June 2011.

OECD MSTI — OECD, *Main Science and Technology Indicators*, 2012.

OECD PD — OECD, *Patent Database*, July 2011.

OECD PISA — OECD, *PISA 2009 database*, 2010.

OECD Scoreboard — OECD, *Science, Technology and Industry: Scoreboard 2007*, OECD, 2007.

Pacey 1991 — Arnold Pacey, *Technology in World Civilization*, The MIT Press, 1991.

Pettis 2011 — Michael Pettis, "China's Economy is Headed for a Slowdown", *Wall Street Journal*, 10 August 2011.

Pomeranz 2000 — Kenneth Pomeranz, *The Great Divergence: Europe, China, and the Making of the Modern World Economy*, Princeton University Press, 2000.

Prasad 2009 — Eswar S. Prasad, "Is the Chinese growth miracle built to last?", *China Economic Review*, 20: 103-123, 2009.

Prasad 2011 — Eswar Prasad, "Rebalancing Growth in Asia", *International Finance*, 14(1): 27-66, 2011.

Rawski 2008 — Thomas G. Rawski, "Can China Sustain Rapid Growth Despite Flawed Institutions?", presentation delivered to the *Sixth International Symposium of the Center for China-US Cooperation*, University of Denver, 30-31 May 2008.

Rawski 2008b — Evelyn S. Rawski and Thomas G. Rawski, "China's Economic Development and Global Interactions in the Long Run", paper prepared for the Harvard-Hitotsubashi-Warwick Confernce *Economic Change Around the Indian Ocean in the Very Long Run*, Venice, 22-24 July 2008.

Rawski 2011 — Thomas G. Rawski, "Human Resources and China's Long Economic Boom", *Asia Policy*, 12: 33-78, July 2011.

RIAA 2011 — Recording Industry Association of America Shipment Database, accessed at www.riaa.org.

Saxenian 2006 — Annalee Saxenian, *The New Argonauts: Regional Advantage in the Global Economy*, Harvard University Press, 2006.

Schott 2008 — P. Schott, "The Relative Sophistication of Chinese Exports," *Economic Policy*, 53: 5-49.

Screen Australia 2011 — Screen Australia, *Australia & the World: International Comparisons*, accessed at screenaustralia.gov.au.

SED 2010 — NSF, *2007 Survey of Earned Doctorates*, *2008 Survey of Earned Doctorates*, and *2009 Survey of Earned Doctorates*, data accessed at www.nsf.gov.

Shi 2010 — Yigong Shi and Yi Rao, "China's Research Culture", *Science*, 329 (5996):1128, 3 September 2010.

SJTU 2012 — Shanghai Jiao Ton University, *Academic Ranking of World Universities 2012*, accessed at www.arwu.org.

Slane 2010 — Daniel Slane et al., "2010 Report to Congress", *US-China Economic and Security Review Commission*, US Government Printing Office, 2010.

Turner 1921 — Frederick Jackson Turner, *The Frontier in American History*, New York: Henry Holt and Company, 1921.

UN 2011 — United Nations, *National Accounts Main Aggregates Database*, accessed at www.unstats.un.org/snaama.

USITO 2010 — US Information Technology Organisation, *Written Comments to the US Government Interagency Trade Policy Staff Committee in Response to Federal Register Notice Regarding China's Compliance with its Accession Commitments to the World Trade Organisation (WTO)*, 27 September, 2010.

Wadhwa 2007 — Vivek Wadhwa, AnnaLee Saxenian, Ben Rissing, and Gary Gereffi, "America's New Immigrant Entrepreneurs", *Master of Engineering Management Program, Duke University; School of Information, U.C. Berkeley*, January 2007.

Waldron 1983 — Arthur N. Waldron, "The Problem of the Great Wall of China", *Harvard Journal of Asiatic Studies*, 43 (2): 643-663, December 1983.

Wang 2010 — Zhi Wang and Whang-Jin Wei, "What Accounts for the Rising Sophistication of China's Exports", in Eds. Robert Feenstra and Shang-Jin Wei, *China's Growing Role in World Trade*, The University of Chicago Press, 2010.

Wang 2010b — Shirley S. Wang, "China Entices Scientists to Return Home", *Wall Street Journal*, 18 November 2010.

WB 2011 — World Bank, *World DataBank: World Development Indicators & Global Development Finance*, data accessed at www.worldbank.org/ ddp/home.do.

WB KAM — World Bank, *Knowledge Assessment Methodology*, data accessed at www.worldbank. org/kam.

WEO 2011 — International Monetary Fund, *World Economic Outlook Database*, April 2011.

Wessner 2011 — Charles W. Wessner and the Committee on Comparative National Innovation Policies, *Building the 21ˢᵗ Century: US China Cooperation on Science, Technology, and Innovations*, NAP, 2011.

WIPO 2010 — WIPO, *World Intellectual Property Indicators*, 2010.

WIPO 2011 — WIPO, *World Intellectual Property Indicators*, 2011.

WOK 2011 — *Web of Knowledge*, Thomson Reuters, 2011.

WSJ 2011 — Siobhan Gorman and Julian E. Barnes, "Cyber Combat: Act of War", *Wall Street Journal*, 31 May 2011.

Wuchty 2007 — Stefan Wuchty, Benjamin Jones, and Brian Uzzi — "The Increasing Dominance of Teams in Production of Knowledge", *Science*, 316:1036, 18 May 2007.

Yearbook 2009 — National Bureau of Statistics, *China Statistical Yearbook 2009*, China Statistical Press, October 2009.

Yearbook 2011 — National Bureau of Statistics, *China Statistical Yearbook 2011*, China Statistical Press, October 2011.